H&R BLOCK'S

H&R BLOCK'S

TAX RELIEF

by Henry W. Bloch with Michael Shook

ANDREWS AND MCMEEL
A Universal Press Syndicate Company
Kansas City

Library of Congress Catalog Card Number: 95-77564

ISBN: 0-8362-0556-1

Attention: Schools and Businesses

Andrews and McMeel books are available at quantity discounts with bulk purchase for educational, business, or sales promotional use. For information, please write to Special Sales Department, Andrews and McMeel, 4900 Main Street, Kansas City, Missouri 64112.

Acknowledgments

Collecting stories in *Tax Relief* required the cooperation of many people. After all, the anecdotes you are about to read represent the assorted experiences of H&R Block tax preparers over a period of more than forty years. To gather these diverse and entertaining stories involved communicating throughout our network of tax preparers for the purpose of recording and writing their tales. In an organization our size, this is no easy task. In the process of preparing the manuscript, we had to decline many more stories than we accepted—for a variety of reasons.

Nonetheless, we thank all who submitted a story, and, in particular, the following whose stories appear in the book: Darrel Bofamy, Robert L. Boyer, Donna Brown, Don Burg, Carole Cameron, Joni Cochran, Rich Enchura, Al Gallagher, Carme Gregory, Joanne Glantz, Dick Grate, Clare Gustina, Bill Hamilton, Janice Henn, Mary Kebler, Michelle Lamberg, Renee Large, Bob Lougen, Nelson Manare, Joan McClain, Michael W. Miller, Jerry Misiewicz, Karen Moss, Deborah L. Mount, Linda Murphy, Lee Noble, Gail S. Parker, June Payne, Winn Perry, Carole Pettitt, David Pham, Larry Reamy, Carolyn Riggins, Larry Roames, Joni Schiller, Bernie Smith, William Snyder, Bill Stratemeier, Jean Thompson, Steve Tressler, Judy Van-Blarcom, Garnett Walker, Rusty Wallower (who not only told a few stories but also helped with the reviewing and editing process), Cathy Young, and Sheila Young.

A special thank-you to several people in H&R Block's world headquarters in Kansas City, who helped to coordinate, edit, and guide the book. At the top of this list is Marti Johnson—in working with Marti, we found out why H&R Block field people love her so much! Cynthia Weber Scherb, the company's legal counsel, did a superb job with our contracts. Also many thank-yous to Tom Bloch, Harry Buckley, and Tom Zimmerman, who had a hand in this project from start to finish.

We are also grateful to Maggie Abel in Columbus, Ohio, who transcribed interviews and helped organize and edit the manuscript. A special thanks to our literary agent, Al Zuckerman, and at Andrews and McMeel, we are grateful to have the pleasure of working with Donna Martin, a wonderful editor, and Katie Mace, an extraordinary production editor.

As you can see, it took a real team effort to put this book together. We are deeply grateful to all of you for your contributions.

Introduction

To many taxpayers, a book on income taxes would be more of a horror book than a humor book!

No wonder when the publication of this book was first announced, a friend asked me, "What's so funny about taxes?"

Little did he know! During my forty years in the tax-preparation business, I've seen stress, deadlines, and pure red tape cause some folks to do and say a lot of pretty funny things! What's more, it seems the tax preparers I meet usually have a favorite story to tell me. Each time we get together at H&R Block seminars and meetings, many delightful anecdotes are certain to be exchanged. And with more than forty-five thousand tax preparers in our organization, serving more than fifteen million taxpayers every year, we have accumulated enough stories to fill a book!

Between creative excuses for late returns, highly innovative deductions, and what some people think is good old common sense in filing a return, you don't have to be a tax preparer to see the whimsical side of my business. And when you've heard as many funny stories as I have, you don't have to be a Bob Hope or a Robin Williams to know there's a large audience out there that enjoys a good laugh about income taxes. Remember, you don't have to feel guilty about laughing about it. Nobody's going to report you to the IRS if you do!

In compiling this book, the hardest challenge was deciding which rib-ticklers to include. Soon we realized that *Tax Relief* had taken on a life of its own, going beyond anything ever written on the topic. To add to that, in our archives, we came across some fascinating, little-known tax facts, tidbits that are sprinkled throughout the book.

The people at H&R Block think you'll enjoy our collection of humorous stories about taxes. Of course, remember, we're tax preparers. And we see an interesting side of taxpayers they might not have realized was showing! So read on, and *you be the judge!*

Although the stories in this book are based on actual incidents, the names of people and places have been changed to protect the innocent (as well as the guilty).

Only Your Doctor and Tax Preparer Know for Sure

It was late March 1982 when Ellen Davidson, a new tax preparer for H&R Block in Houston, introduced herself to her new client, Sherry Jones. Mrs. Jones, a slender, attractive woman, appeared to be in her mid-forties.

"Good afternoon! I'm Ellen Davidson. It's a pleasure to meet you, ma'am."

"I'm Sherry Jones," the woman buoyantly replied. "I'm having some problems with my return, and so I decided to let a pro help me."

After conducting the usual interview and doing the necessary paperwork, Ellen carefully glanced over Mrs. Jones's return. She couldn't help noticing the birth date, January 10, 1920. This would make the young-looking Mrs. Jones sixty-two years old! She glanced up at the lady in surprise, then back down at

the paper. Maybe her client put down the wrong date, Ellen thought. It sometimes happens.

"It says here you were born in 1920, Mrs. Jones." Ellen said. "Evidently, you—"

"No, it's correct," said the woman, smiling broadly.

Ellen looked at her in astonishment. "Why, you don't look a day over forty! Did you discover the fountain of youth? What's your secret?"

"Well," said the woman with a hushed voice and a twinkle in her eye, "let's give credit where credit is due. I've been using Mary Kay skin-care products for the past fifteen years, I attend aerobics twice a day, and I follow a very healthy diet."

"Wow!" exclaimed Ellen. She thought of the cobwebs on her stationary bike and the fast food she had had for lunch. "I can't begin to tell you how many women come in here to write off their nose jobs and face-lifts. You're lucky you didn't have to go through any of that."

Mrs. Jones looked up in surprise. "Are you telling me cosmetic surgery is tax deductible?"

"It can be," Ellen said.

Mrs. Jones's mouth dropped, her eyebrows met her hairline, and her eyes widened. Suddenly vanity flew out the window. She cleared her throat, as if gathering courage.

"Actually, last year I had a nose job by Dr. Meyers. Then I looked so good I decided to get a face-lift and have those dark bags under my eyes removed. After that, I thought, let's go for it all, Sherry! So I had a liposuction and a tummy tuck this past November."

"Do you have the receipts at home?" Ellen asked.

"Do I?" Mrs. Jones exclaimed. "What time do you open in the morning?"

The next day, Mrs. Jones returned. She presented a year's worth of cosmetic surgery bills, totaling over $16,000—at a time when cosmetic surgery was deductible.

According to Luke

Even back in biblical days, taxes were a taxing subject. In the Book of Luke it is written: "There went out a decree from Caesar Augustus that all the world should be taxed."

Just as Egypt had done in previous centuries, in the year of the birth of Christ Caesar Augustus decreed that a mandatory census be taken. In the census, every male over the age of fourteen and every woman over the age of twelve was required to list his or her possessions as well as all sources of income. Evidently, the Romans respected their senior citizens—they were exempt from these requirements.

The Roman tax collectors in the Bible are referred to as publicans; these officials had the authority to negotiate a tax in advance with each taxpayer; a portion of what they collected was paid to Rome. A publican had an incentive to do a good job. Exactly how much he collected above or below a certain fixed sum was either his profit or loss!

Throughout the provinces, the Roman property tax ranged from 25 percent to 33 percent of a crop's yield. There was also a "poll tax," consisting of a uniform head tax, income tax, and other personal taxes. There is no way to determine the going rate of taxation at that time since each publican could determine how much he collected from taxpayers in his jurisdiction.

The Jews were a favorite target of the Roman tax collectors; because they came from well-defined families that could be traced to certain ancestral areas, it was easy for the Romans to identify them. Hence, it was a Roman law that every Jew must remain in a location where the tax collector could find him or her during the tax season. In the Book of Luke, Mary and Joseph, who were members of the House of David, had been required to travel a distance of sixty miles by donkey in their return to Bethlehem from Nazareth.

The Work of Fiction

Betty Anderson was excited to have a prolific and oft-published author as her client.

"What do you consider your best work of fiction?" she asked.

The author didn't hesitate. Tongue in cheek, he replied, "You're looking at it—my tax return."

The Stone

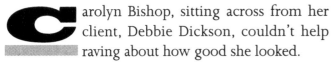arolyn Bishop, sitting across from her client, Debbie Dickson, couldn't help raving about how good she looked.

"I love your new haircut," Carolyn marveled. "And you look absolutely stunning in that outfit."

"I should," the fifty-five-year-old woman answered. "It cost me $800. Now look at this. What do you think of this four-carat diamond?" Debbie boasted, proudly extending her right hand.

"Is it an engagement ring?"

"No, I bought it for myself!"

"Wow! You make that kind of money in tips?" Carolyn asked. "Maybe I should be a waitress. Think there'll be any openings at the restaurant starting in May?"

"Actually, my uncle died," Debbie confessed.

"I'm sorry to hear that," said Carolyn. "He must have left you a lot of money."

"Around $15,000—with only one string attached. He asked me to purchase a stone in his memory. Well," she replied with a twinkle in her eye, "you're looking at it."

TAX TRIVIA

Early Tariffs . . .

It was the Arabs who first imposed a toll on ships passing into and out of the Mediterranean. They did this in El Tarifa, near Gibraltar, and this is where the word for import tax (tariff) is derived.

Even Your Tax Preparer Witnesses Miracles

For the last four years, Judy and John Handy had taken their tax work to the H&R Block office in Michigan's Upper Peninsula. Money problems were no stranger to them. Just that previous year, John's small construction company had operated in the red, and Judy was laid off from the lumber mill where she worked as a secretary.

It was the beginning of tax season, and the Handys were back again; as usual, they requested Dave Schultz.

"John! Judy! How's it going, guys?" Dave asked, giving them a warm greeting.

"Well, to tell you truth, Dave," John said, "I'm afraid we're filing separate tax returns this year. You see, Judy and I got a divorce earlier this month."

Dave was taken aback by the news. What a shame,

he thought. The attractive, thirtysomething couple appeared to get along so well.

Just as Dave was about to offer his condolences, Judy went back out to the car to get her briefcase.

"This is none of my business," Dave said, "but you both seemed so good for each other. What happened, John?"

"Well, our money situation really soured me, Dave," he said. "I figured maybe I could do better with someone else."

Dave's jaw dropped. What did John mean by "do better"?

With a heavy heart, he finished their returns and wished them both the best of luck.

The following season John came in again—this time with a well-dressed elderly lady carrying a small poodle. Just as Dave was about to put his foot in his mouth and say, "You must be John's mother," John introduced his new wife, Edith.

"How do you do?" Dave gasped.

The elderly woman coughed a few times, tightening her grip on the miniature poodle, and responded in a raspy voice. "Fine, thanks. John has told me what a wonderful job you do, young man."

Dave went through her records and discovered she was an extremely wealthy woman. But based on her high medical expenses, it was a good guess that John's new bride did not have long to live.

Then it hit him. Looking up at his smug client, Dave could almost see the dollar signs in John's eyes. How could he do it? Dave wondered to himself. How could he leave Judy for a rich old lady who was about to cash in her chips?

Okay, Dave, get a grip on yourself, he thought. You're only their tax preparer. Finish the return and get on with your day. This is none of your business.

When Dave finished their return and sent them out the door, he couldn't help noticing the spring in John's step.

The following year, John and Edith came back to

have their taxes prepared—only this time it was much different! John seemed twenty years older, while Edith looked like she had discovered the fountain of youth. Her hair looked fuller, she had put on some weight, and there was a definite bloom in her cheeks.

"The doctor's latest treatment worked!" she said excitedly. "Even the doctors are amazed. If I take good care of myself, they say I could live to be a hundred years old."

John sat hunched over in his chair, stroking the poodle on his lap. "Yeah," he mumbled, "it's a miracle."

The Bible Says ...

Tithe, according to the Bible, or a tenth of the produce, was due as an annual tax. Likewise the standard Roman land tax paid by landowners and lessees of public land was one-tenth (decuma). The personal tax levied by the Egyptian pharaohs was a little steeper—it ran about 18 percent of the produce of each household.

In Egypt and Mesopotamia, the temples of the god-kings were used for storage and distribution of grain collected as tax payments. The biblical story about Joseph describes how his dreams influenced the king to set up a seven-year reserve for a predicted famine. To realize this surplus of grain, the peasants were taxed dearly. This may well be the earliest recorded example of economic planning through taxation.

Can I Take Off My Clothes?

An attractive young lady walked into an H&R Block office in Baltimore to get her taxes prepared one busy morning during tax season. Even though ten other people sat in the reception area, with April 15 right around the corner, she decided to wait.

Twenty minutes later, the receptionist called her name.

"Elle McFall, we're ready for you."

Elle looked up from beneath her long eyelashes.

"Mr. Baxter will see you now, Elle," the receptionist said.

Putting the latest edition of *Cosmopolitan* back on the table, Elle was greeted by veteran tax preparer Tony Baxter. In his entire eighteen years with the firm, Tony had rarely seen such a beautiful woman in the waiting room.

"Well, good morning. You must be Ms. McFall. Sorry about the delay. But as you can see we've been swamped all morning."

She smiled a beautiful smile. "It was actually kind of nice sitting down for a few minutes," she said. "I'm on my feet all day at work."

"Exactly what do you do, Ms. McFall?"

"I'm a flight attendant. And, please, call me Elle," she said. They sat down at Tony's desk.

"Is it possible for me to take off my clothes?" she asked in a very serious tone.

"Er, excuse me. What did you say, Elle?"

"My clothes, Tony. Can I take them off?"

"Well, er . . . gosh, uh, Elle, while we pride ourselves in a complete and thorough interview, well, ah, most clients are more comfortable fully clothed."

"Mr. Baxter! I'm talking about my stewardess uniforms. Are they deductible?"

With his face blush red and his eyes fixed firmly on the desk before him, Tony mumbled, "I don't see why not, ma'am."

Graduated Taxes

The concept of taxes being based on the taxpayer's ability to pay—with progressive rates—goes way back. Long ago, it was recognized as unfair to tax the poor at the same rate as the rich.

More than three thousand years ago, the Indian sage Manu espoused this principle when he said, "To make the burden of taxes equal ... is not affected by a mere numerical proportion. The man who is taxed to the amount of one tenth ... of an income of one hundred rupees per annum, is taxed far more severely than the man who is taxed an equal proportion of an income of one thousand rupees, and to a prodigious bigness more severely than the man who is taxed an equal proportion of ten thousand rupees per annum."

This principle of fairness was carried into the Middle Ages in England where it was considered unfair to tax the rich man and the peasant at the same rate. Note, for example, that the poll tax of 1377 taxed the Duke of Lancaster at a rate 520 times that of the peasant.

A Good Excuse for a Speedy Refund Check

n elderly gentleman walked very slowly into an H&R Block office in Houston, Texas.

"I want to speak to one of them preparers right now," he demanded.

"What is your name, sir?" the receptionist asked.

"You didn't hear me ask for your name, now did you?" he retorted. "I want to speak to one of them right now."

Although half a dozen people were before him in the waiting room, the receptionist accommodated his request. It would have been poor judgment, she thought, to let the cantankerous man disturb everyone else.

The next available preparer, Debra Brown, came over to the reception area.

"How can I help you, sir?"

"Well, ma'am, I been tryin' to get ahold of them IRS folk for over two weeks now, and I still can't get through. Will you help me?"

"Maybe I'll try. What exactly do you need to speak to them about?"

"I been waitin' for that dang refund check an awful long time. I want them to ship it to me now!" the man screamed hoarsely.

"It should arrive early next month, sir." Debra explained in a gentle voice. "It's perfectly normal for it to take this long. Let's be patient and remember that the IRS has to process tens of millions of returns this time of year."

"Oh, yeah? Well, how many ninety-three-year-old men do those folks have to prepare money for? I've been giving them money my entire life, and I want to make sure I get that refund check while I'm still among the living!"

Only Your Tax Preparer May Know the Truth

It was 8:00 A.M. sharp on April 15, and Laura was getting ready for an extremely busy day. She had just downed her first cup of coffee when the telephone rang.

"Good morning, H&R Block," Laura said.

The lady on the phone seemed anxious. "I called yesterday and talked to Todd Collins about picking up my daughter's return for her. She's overseas for a little while, so I thought I'd come by and pick it up for her."

"Yes?" Laura questioned.

"Well, that Todd character wouldn't give it to me. There is no reason in the world why I shouldn't be allowed to pick up my baby's return, is there?"

Feeling a little mystified, Laura said, "Well, let me check with Todd, and I'll call you right back."

The digital clock on Todd's desk read 8:05 when Laura approached his desk.

"I am sorry to bother you, Todd, but there's something I need to run by you."

"No problem, Laura," he said.

"Todd, I just got a call from a mother who was quite upset. She talked to you yesterday about wanting to come in to pick up her daughter's return."

"Yes, I know exactly who you mean, but be sure not to give it to her."

"What's the big deal, Todd? She's all worked up. Why not?"

"The daughter's a model in Paris," he said. "She gave me specific instructions in a letter: 'Under no circumstances is my mother allowed to see my return.'"

"Oh, I guess she doesn't want her mother to see how much she earns," Laura rationalized.

"Not quite," Todd said. "It has to do with her medical expenses on a Schedule A."

"Oh no!" Laura said. "Is it some kind of terrible illness she doesn't want her mom to know about?"

Todd said. "Save your sympathy, Laura. It's just that, to model her bathing suits better, the daughter had a breast enlargement, which is deductible in her profession."

At this, Laura laughed out loud.

"Cut it out, Laura! Women do this all the time," Todd said.

"I know, Todd. But when they see each other again, don't you think her own mother would notice something—er—different?"

"That's the point, Laura. She doesn't think her mom will even notice," said Todd. "She told me she didn't get her money's worth!"

Roman Tax on Urine

Back in the days of the Roman Empire, tax collectors were always dreaming up ways to generate revenue for the government. In the first century A.D., for example, Emperor Vespasian levied a tax on urine—that is, when it was used as a cleaning or leather-tanning agent.

A Dangerous Return

In a San Francisco strip mall, a young woman walked into an H&R Block office on Friday five minutes before closing time. Amy, the receptionist, asked, "Is there something we can do for you?"

The lady pulled a yard-long two-by-four from behind her back.

Terrified, Amy put up her arms to defend herself, shouting, "We don't have any money in the office! I may have some in my—"

"No, no, you've got it all wrong!" said the woman. "It's my boyfriend's," she explained, waving the board.

Amy winced and instinctively raised her arms in defense.

"My boyfriend is working overtime at the construction site. He asked me to bring in his tax stuff for him before the office closed today."

Amy took a few deep breaths and tried to stop shaking. "Do you mean to tell me that's his tax information—on the board?"

"This is it," the girlfriend answered.

She then displayed the board to Amy. "Mark Whitfield" was scribbled on the side with a carpenter's pencil. Looking a little closer, Amy saw a social security number and other information underneath his name, and some folded papers stapled to the reverse side. "He didn't have any paper at the job site," the young woman began to explain. Not letting his job responsibilities stop him, Mark had stapled his W2 to the two-by-four with a staple gun and filled in his other information on the other side of the board!

You're in the Army Now

In ancient Greece and Rome, taxes were paid with personal service. Every male citizen was a soldier, required to serve in war and supply his own weapons.

You Can Run, but You Can't Hide from Your Tax Preparer

Back in 1982, a pretty young lady walked into an H&R Block office in Phoenix, Arizona. Ted Haynes was the lucky preparer assigned to her.

"Good morning, Mrs. O'Brien," he said, shaking her hand.

"Please, call me Jean," she said in a deep, sexy voice. She gave his hand a squeeze that made his fingers ache.

That's one firm handshake, he thought to himself.

"Okay," he said, "let's see what you've got here."

One at a time she handed him six folders containing neatly folded forms. What a breeze, he thought.

As Ted booted up his computer to enter the information, he glanced over her first W2 form, noticing that the last name was the same throughout, but there were different first names. "Pardon me, Jean," he said. "I'm confused. It says here that this tax return is for John O'Brien. It may be necessary for your husband to be present to sign the forms."

"John is not my husband!" she said, her voice suddenly going hoarse.

"Well, I'm sorry, Jean. But you can't sign for an ex-husband or brother either."

"He is neither my ex-husband nor my brother!" she said.

"Whoever John O'Brien is, he will need to sign his own tax return. Kindly tell him he'll have to come in and sign it personally."

Jean cleared her throat and got to the point. "He is here."

Suddenly it dawned on Ted—the deep voice, the broad shoulders, the firm handshake. In the true H&R Block tradition, he recovered quickly.

"Well then, John—I mean Jean—all you have to do is put down your Jean, I mean, John Hancock right here, and you'll be on your way."

Taxpayers Beware

Considered to be every taxpayer's worst nightmare—and no matter how careful you are, you can't avoid it—is the audit done by the Taxpayer Compliance Measurement Program. Of the 2 percent of the returns audited in 1995, a record 153,000 were chosen at random to be subjected to a TCMP audit.

How bad is it? Even IRS agents refer to it as the bureaucratic equivalent of a rubber-hose interrogation. While the typical audit focuses on one or two items, and many are conducted by mail, this audit really gets down to business. IRS auditors review everything, concentrating on the taxpayer's lifestyle in search of any shred of evidence of unreported income.

These auditors ask questions like: How are you able to dine at so many expensive restaurants? How can you afford the clothes you wear? How did you come up with the money to pay for your kids' education? They also require you to verify unidentified bank deposits to prove they weren't hidden income.

A TCMP audit easily takes five to six times as long as a normal exam. And why does the IRS conduct a TCMP? Interestingly, it isn't done to collect more revenue but instead to gather more data to update its audit-scoring system!

The Weatherman

ne beautiful April morning when not a cloud was in the sky, everyone in Memphis seemed to be enjoying the sudden burst of warm weather.

It was nearly noon on this glorious Saturday, and Lisa Johnson wished she could be far away from the office. But with one week to go before April 15, she still had a long day ahead of her. Such was the life of an H&R Block tax preparer during tax season.

She had just completed a return for Hugh Green, who happened to be one of the most popular weathermen in the area. "Well, tell me, Hugh," Lisa asked, "What's your forecast for this afternoon?"

"You can say rain is an absolute certainty, Lisa," Green answered.

"You gotta be kidding," she said. "Look outside. Are you sure about rain?"

"Yes, ma'am," Green shot back. "Absolutely."

"How can you be so positive?"

"I got my car washed this morning, I have a tee-time at one, and my wife is planning to do some gardening."

TAX TRIVIA

Miscellaneous . . .

1.) *Tax Time—the time of year when they tell you what to do with the money you already did something with.*

2.) *I voted for change, and guess what? After taxes, that's all I have left.*

3.) *The deli owner was audited this year—turns out not all of his deductions were kosher.*

The Bathroom Appointment

It was Rachael Jones's first year as a tax preparer with H&R Block. It was also that time of year—the height of tax season!

Although she had worked at the office for several months, Rachael had never experienced the fast pace of the month of April. But she had heard stories from other preparers about the long hours and hard work, and now it was her turn to experience it firsthand.

"Wow!" Rachael exclaimed to her coworker Sheryl, after a hectic Monday morning. "I feel like I just learned how to ride a bicycle, and I'm suddenly racing in the Tour de France!"

The two of them talked about work during their quick lunch in the back room. Rachael was given some much-needed advice about what to expect when preparing returns of clients who came in so close to April 15. Afterward, she headed back to her desk for her one o'clock appointment.

"Good afternoon, Mr. Baxter," Rachael cheerfully greeted her client.

"Good afternoon. Thanks so much for squeezing me into your busy day," Baxter replied. "This is the only time I could come in this week, and I desperately need tax help."

"I'm glad I can help," Rachael said. I actually could have used a longer lunch hour, she thought, with all that coffee I drank this morning.

Before sitting down, she said, "Excuse me, Mr. Baxter, but I must visit the ladies room before I go on with your taxes. I'll be back in a couple of seconds."

"No problem," he said. "You're the one that slid me into your busy schedule on such short notice."

Rachael passed Sheryl's desk, giving her a big wink as she hurried into the restroom. After washing her hands and discarding her crumpled paper towel, she discovered that the door was stuck. Okay, she thought, who's the wise guy holding the door? She tried the door again, to no avail.

"Hello out there! I'm in here!" she said, thinking someone might be trying to get in at the same time.

"Hello, someone! Please help me get the door open!" Her tone turned from embarrassment to nervousness when she realized no one was struggling on the other side. The door was just plain stuck.

"Someone, please help me! Sheryl, are you there?" shouted Rachael. Thinking about how much noise she was making made Rachael think about the embarrassment she'd face when she finally got out. Working nearby, Sheryl finally realized what was going on and excused herself from her client.

"Rachael, is that you?"

"Yes, it's me. Get me out!"

Like Laurel and Hardy, the two of them struggled with the doorknob—until it finally broke off!

"Oh, no! The handle didn't just fall off, did it?" Rachael asked hysterically.

By this time, the noise had attracted the entire office. She could hear muffled laughter.

"Sheryl, are you still there?" Rachael asked in desperation.

"Yes, I'm still here. Hang tight, I'm going to call the handyman. He should be here shortly."

By this time, Mr. Baxter had come to see what was going on.

Through the door, he asked "Rachael, are you okay?"

Despite his sincere tone, Rachael was too embarrassed to reply.

"Rachael?" he called again. "I know you're in there." He sounded like a baby-sitter looking for a small child during a game of hide-and-seek.

"Yes, Mr. Baxter, I'm in here. I'm sorry, but the knob broke off, and I'm stuck for a while. Can we finish your taxes another time?"

"Actually, since I'm here now, I'd like to get it over with, Rachael. Can I just slip the papers under the door and get them done now?"

At first, Rachael thought her client was joking, but after a long pause, she realized his seriousness. "Good thinking!" she said, responding to her sense of duty. "Might as well not waste any time in here."

Rachael finished Mr. Baxter's return by using the toilet bowl lid as a table, while communicating with him through the keyhole in the door.

Oh, IRA!

William O'Brien was wearing a Notre Dame baseball cap and a Fighting Irish T-shirt when he walked into the H&R Block office in Princeton, New Jersey.

"Can I help you, sir?" asked the friendly receptionist.

"Yes, I need some help with my taxes. I'm having a bloody hard time doing them on my own," the man said. The receptionist couldn't quite place his heavy accent.

"Take a seat and the next available preparer will help you."

Before the man could even pick up a magazine, Robert Jenkins came out to the lobby to greet him.

"I'm ready for you, Mr. O'Brien," Robert said in a heavy New Jersey accent.

While going through the client's files, Robert came to a folder labeled "Individual Retirement Account."

Waving the folder, Robert asked, "When was the last time you made an IRA contribution?"

The man stood up angrily and snapped, "What bloody business is that of yours? Just because I'm an Irishman, you assume I support the Irish Republican Army. Why don't you just mind your own—"

Robert interrupted him midsentence. "I'm sorry, Mr. O'Brien," he said sincerely. "I was talking about your Individual Retirement Account. I should have said that to begin with."

When Mr. O'Brien saw the folder Robert was holding, he looked down at the ground, his face beet-red. "Please accept my apologies, Mr. Jenkins. I hope I didn't offend you! With all that is going on in the world, that's kind of a touchy subject for me to talk about these days."

Priority Paperwork

Laura Hayes worked at the Savannah H&R Block office for one month, and although she thoroughly enjoyed her job, as hard as she tried, the new receptionist made more than her share of mistakes—especially when doing little favors for veteran tax preparer Jim Richards.

"Laura, could you please file these papers that Walter Sullivan just dropped off?" Jim asked.

"No problem, Jim," she said—accidentally putting the manila envelope on her desk with the rest of the outgoing mail.

Three days later Walter called Jim, wondering why the papers were sent back to him.

"I'm sorry, Walter. It must have been a mistake," Jim said sympathetically. "Would you mind bringing the papers back to our office when you're next in our neck of the woods?"

"Well, I'm coming to your part of town early tomorrow morning," Walter replied. "There's a lot I'd like to get done around the farm before the heat of the day, so I'll be dropping it off before sunrise."

"Just drop it in the drop box at the front door. And again, Walter, sure am sorry about the inconvenience."

Laura was the first one in the office that morning. She looked in the mail box and saw the same manila envelope she had sent out earlier in the week. Wow, that's funny, she thought. I wonder why the post office brought it back. Maybe I didn't have enough stamps on it the first time. She double-checked the address, stuffed the whole manila envelope in a new envelope, reweighed and stamped it, and out it went that same morning! How's that for efficiency?

The Wildlife Fund

young college student at the University of West Virginia came to an H&R Block office to get his very first tax return prepared. After he sat a few minutes in the waiting room, the receptionist called his name.

"David Kanes, we're ready for you," said the receptionist. No answer. "David? David?"

David was sitting back in his chair with his legs propped up on the magazine table. His head was swaying along with the heavy metal blaring from his Walkman earphones. Even the others in the waiting room could hear the music. Finally an elderly man sitting next to him gave the young man a nudge. Dave stood up abruptly, ripping his earphones off.

"Wow, are you guys ready for me already?" he asked with a frown. "I was just startin' to relax."

The elderly man's white eyebrows squinched together, making a small ragged mountain in the middle of his forehead. "Boy," he whispered to the pregnant woman sitting next to him, "when I was a kid I had no time to relax like that. I worked on our farm fourteen hours a day—"

"We could let someone go ahead of you if you would like, Mr. Kanes," the receptionist offered.

Remembering he was "hanging out" in a tax preparation office, David calmly said, "No, it's all right. Let's get it over with."

The preparer came out to introduce himself. Once they were seated at his desk, the preparer asked David a series of questions, reviewed his papers, and mentioned to his client that he could elect the option to donate to the West Virginia Wildlife Fund.

"Absolutely!" the college student said with a chuckle. "Where's the party?"

Not quite understanding what he meant, the preparer said, "You have the choice to donate to the West Virginia Wildlife Fund. Are you interested in helping out West Virginia's wildlife?"

"Absolutely," the college student replied. "Everyone should have more wild life!"

Irish Window Tax

In the late 1600s, Ireland enforced a "window tax." Home owners were assessed according to the number of windows in their houses!

Dead in Bed

Jay Shore had prepared the Blooms' taxes for the past seven years. He'd grown very close to the elderly couple; they reminded him of his own grandparents. So he found it especially hard to watch Mr. and Mrs. Bloom's health begin to deteriorate in their old age. The Blooms were one of the affluent families in the community, yet they lived as modestly as schoolteachers.

One afternoon Lenore Bloom called the office, insisting on speaking to Jay.

"Jay, I don't know what I am going to do," Lenore said. "Harry had a stroke this morning and the doctor says it's a serious one."

Jay consoled her until she felt more calm. For the next several months he kept close contact with the couple, offering to do small favors, such as running errands. Since Harry was bedridden, Lenore designated herself as his caregiver. Jay tried to convince her to hire some help, but the independent Lenore stubbornly insisted on doing everything herself.

As time went on, Lenore suspected everyone was after the family's enormous estate. She grew more and more withdrawn and wary of others who tried to offer assistance. The only person she really trusted was Jay; she called him constantly to seek his advice.

"Jay, could you look over our water bill to make sure the water company is not overcharging us? It's $13 more than last July's bill."

Her questions boggled Jay's mind. She receives tens of thousands of dollars in dividends each month; how could she let such minor expenditures worry her? Over time, Jay involuntarily became her lawyer, handyman, electrician, and psychologist. Day and night she called, asking more and more ludicrous questions.

One day Mrs. Bloom called the office while Jay was away. The receptionist assured her that Jay would return her call as soon as possible. Several hours passed before Jay returned her call.

"Jay, I've got terrible news."

What is it? Jay wondered, recalling past so-called emergency calls she had made to him. Your water heater is leaking? Your answering machine is losing messages?

"What's the matter, Mrs. Bloom?" asked a sincere but weary Jay.

"Brace yourself, Jay. It's terrible," she said in a low voice.

"Calm down, Mrs. Bloom. Take a deep breath and tell me what happened.

"Harry is dead in bed," she said with a little sob.

"What are you saying? Do you mean your husband has died?"

"Yes, Jay. What do I do?"

Obviously shaken, Jay took a long pause to catch his breath. Finally, he asked the widow, "Did you call for an ambulance, Mrs. Bloom?"

"No, I didn't want to do a thing until I talked to you first!"

"Well, Mrs. Bloom, the first thing to do is to call an ambulance. I'll be right over to help you. We'll need to choose a funeral home, and there are some decisions to make about funeral arrangements . . ."

After Jay hung up the phone, he sat there, stunned. He pulled his business card out of his wallet and stared at it. Amazingly, in large bold letters, it still read simply, "Tax Preparer."

Hesitant Deductions

 sharply dressed middle-aged man walked into an H&R Block office in downtown Boston, wanting to get his taxes done as quickly as possible.

"Mr. Shelbourne, we're ready for you," the receptionist announced.

The tax preparer came over. "Good morning, I'm Frank Myers," he said to the distinguished-looking gentleman.

"Yeah, I need some help with my return, but I have a meeting in about a half hour. Can you do it, or should I go somewhere else?"

"It normally takes a little longer than that, Mr. Shelbourne, but I'll see what I can do."

Following a review of the man's various sources of earnings, Frank started working on the deductions.

He began with business deductions. Frank asked, "Mr. Shelbourne, for the deduction on your return, how many business miles do you drive?"

"Lots," he said, as if he didn't have enough time to say more.

"I'm sorry, Mr. Shelbourne, but I need to know how many miles to put on your return."

"My tax preparer in the past just put anything down. Maybe I should go to him?"

"That's up to you, sir. But if I do your return, I need to know what mileage to put down."

"Why don't we get back to that question later," Shelbourne replied.

"Fine," Frank sighed. "And how much did you spend on office supplies this past year?"

"$850," Shelbourne instantly responded.

"Okay, and how much did you give to charities this past year?"

"That's between me and God," Mr. Shelbourne said in a very serious tone.

Frank's patience had reached its limit. "If you're going to claim it on your return, Mr. Shelbourne, it's going to be between you, God, and the IRS."

British Bachelor Tax

In 1695, English law levied a tax on bachelors. At the time, it seemed like a good idea to inspire eligible Englishmen to choose a bride. In 1820, the state of Missouri levied a one-dollar tax on bachelors from ages twenty-one to fifty because they didn't have a wife.

What's My Line?

Sam Marcus nervously sat down at John Wilson's desk. The distinguished-looking man obviously felt ill at ease in the presence of his tax preparer.

In an attempt to relax his client, John said, "Well, here we are, approaching another April 15. I guess we all feel on edge at this time of year."

"Yeah," Marcus answered. "I-I certainly qualify as one of those people."

There was a slight chill in the room, but John couldn't help noticing his client was perspiring.

"Are you all right, sir?"

"As well as can be expected," Marcus said, his voice quavering.

Wow, John thought. I've never seen anyone so nervous in my life. "Would you like a cup of coffee before we get started on your return, sir? It might relax you."

"That would be great," Marcus said with a faint smile.

John filled Marcus's cup only half way, so he wouldn't spill it.

The man was shaking so badly he could hardly put the cup of coffee to his mouth. Half of it spilled on the poor fellow's slacks as he managed to take a sip.

"All right, sir. Let's get started on your return." John then began asking the standard questions for a new client.

"What is your occupation?" John asked.

"Brain surgeon," the man said.

The Beard Tax

In 1702, Russia enacted a tax on men who sported beards.

The Discourteous Police Officer

"I've changed jobs since you did my return last year," Fred Tilson told his tax preparer. "I'm not a salesclerk anymore—now I'm a policeman."

"What made you change occupations, Fred?"

"Oh, I was fired by the store manager," Tilson answered. "They said I was discourteous to customers. I guess I wasn't cut out for sales. I just couldn't accept the fact that the customer was always right."

"Yes, that's a cardinal rule in sales," the tax preparer acknowledged.

"Yeah, but what I like about my new job is that the customer is always wrong."

The Boston Tea Party

In 1773, as a direct result of a British tea tax of three-pence per pound, the Boston Tea Party was thrown. Although the tax was lower than the colonists had been paying, they preferred to smuggle in Dutch tea rather than pay a tax to the British. John Hancock was one of the most prominent smugglers—and he convinced the colonists that if they paid the tea tax, it would result in many more taxes.

Can I Claim My Girlfriend?

man visited an H&R Block office in downtown Los Angeles back in 1965, but he didn't come alone. Accompanying him were two women—a blonde and a brunette—and four children.

"Good morning," the man said to the receptionist. "I need to get some tax help."

"The next preparer will be available in about ten minutes. If you all want to take a seat in the waiting room, we'll call for you when we're ready."

The man sat with his arm around the brunette, while the blonde supervised the children. I guess that's their baby-sitter, the receptionist thought. But why in the world would a couple want to bring along their kids and baby-sitter to this office?

Brian Smith, the next available tax preparer, came out a few minutes later and greeted the small gathering. "Why don't you all come on back to my desk, and we'll get the show under way," he said, making a funny face to the youngest child.

The man followed Brian, with the two women and four kids trailing closely behind. As they were walking down the hallway the man cleared his throat a few times. "I used to do my taxes myself," he began to explain, "but it has gotten a little confusing lately."

"I'm sure we'll figure it out," Brian reassured him.

"Well, you see," said the man, "this is my wife." He pointed to the middle-aged brunette, who responded by blushing and nodding her head. "These are our four kids." Brian smiled.

"And this is my girlfriend," the man continued.

What in the world? Brian thought. His second thought was, why aren't these women at each other's throats?

"I'm not sure if I can do this," the man said, "but I'd like to claim my girlfriend as a dependent, along with the kids."

Brian looked at the man in disbelief.

"You see," the man blurted out, "both my wife and I work full-time, and my girlfriend has no other responsibilities except taking care of the kids and running the house. She has no other income, and I take care of everything for her."

The man was undeniably correct. After Brian checked with the IRS—back in 1965, then it was common to ask the IRS questions—it was confirmed that the man was entitled to file a joint return with his wife, and list his girlfriend and the kids as dependents.

Refunds to All Taxpayers

During the Andrew Jackson administration, the U.S. government accumulated a surplus of $37 million. On June 23, 1836, after some debate, Congress voted to refund the money to the states in proportion to their representation in Congress. The panic of 1837 hit the following year and revenues decreased. Never again was the federal government so generous as to refund a surplus.

Charge!

lvin Carter had spent more than an hour in the H&R Block office, located just across the street from a large Minneapolis shopping mall in the suburbs. Stan Wilson, his tax preparer, took a last look over Carter's return and said, "It looks fine to me, Alvin. All I need are your signatures."

"Signatures?" Carter questioned. "You mean my signature."

"For the electronic filing, I also need Mrs. Carter's."

"Gotcha, Stan, but she's across the street shopping. Is it okay for me to sign her name?"

"Sorry, Alvin, she has to sign it. What time did she say she'd be back?"

"I told her to meet me here in an hour, but once she gets started in a mall, she loses all track of time. She could be there for hours," Alvin sighed.

"I guess you'll just have to be patient and wait her out," Wilson answered.

"I got a better idea," Alvin said. "Mind if I use your phone?"

"You can't call every store in the mall," Carter said. "There are a couple dozen women's shops alone over there."

"That won't be necessary," Alvin replied. "I'm just going to call Visa and Mastercard to cancel her cards. I promise you, once I do, my wife will be right over!"

The Cover Letter

fter completing the tax return form, the tax preparer said to her client, "Well, Mr. Jones, that just about wraps it up."

The polite, older man sitting across her desk was obviously unhappy about something. He reached into his pocket and handed her a neatly typewritten letter. "Would you please attach this letter to my return?" he asked.

The letter, addressed to the IRS, read:

To whom it may concern:

Sir, since my secretary is a refined woman, I cannot ask her to type what I think of the Internal Revenue Service. And I, being a gentleman, cannot say it. You, however, being neither, will understand what I mean.

Sincerely,

Henry Jones

TAX TRIVIA

Taxing Oleomargarine

In 1886, a federal tax was levied on oleomargarine, to protect the butterfat industry. It stayed on the books until 1950!

Don't Call the Police

heila Kelly's most nerve-racking day at the H&R Block Los Angeles Executive Tax Service started quietly—that is, until Karen Miller stormed in.

"Your appointment is not for another hour," the receptionist said.

"You don't understand!" Karen said in a loud voice. "I need to see someone right away!"

"I'm sorry, but you'll need to wait your turn," the receptionist replied.

Karen ignored the receptionist and hurried from desk to desk, looking for somebody to assist her. She finally found a tax preparer who was organizing some papers after finishing with a client.

"Can I help you?" asked Sheila, looking up from her stack of papers.

"Yes," said Karen, laying her paperwork on Sheila's desk. The client kept looking anxiously around the room. She was obviously very nervous.

"Is anything wrong? You seem a little uneasy."

"Yes, I do feel uneasy," she said, breathing heavily. "My ex-husband is following me with a gun."

Suddenly she had the tax preparer's undivided attention. "Did you say your ex-husband is following you with a gun?"

"Yes," Karen said, taking a mighty puff.

"I think we had better do something—right now," Sheila stammered. "Should I call the police?"

"My ex-husband is a police officer!" the woman exclaimed, rolling her eyes.

Luckily, the ex-husband never came into the office. Just the same, Sheila felt a lot more at ease after waving good-bye to Karen after finishing her return.

Does Your Wife Work?

or eleven years, Don Jones had prepared Harold Weiss's tax returns. Don remembered Harold as a single man who owned and operated a small bakery. The old Harold was a constant brooder. A hard-working man, the baker spent a majority of his leisure time watching old movies on his VCR—accompanied only by a TV tray stacked high with cookies and doughnuts from his shop. By some people's standards, Harold's life might have seemed uneventful.

But one day when he came into the H&R Block office in Detroit for his yearly visit, it was a different Harold! He had shed every pound of excess weight. He seemed to prance, not walk, into the office. He was, indeed, a happy man.

"It that you, Harold?" the receptionist asked. "You look marvelous!"

"Thank you, Katherine. Here, I brought in a box of Danish for the office. Would you let Don know I'm here to see him?"

My gosh! Katherine thought. This can't be the same Harold—the semihermit who pays his employees minimum wage. The last time I was at the bakery, I was a nickel short on my muffin—I left hungry! What in the world could have come over him?

When Don came out to the waiting room to greet Harold, he was equally surprised. "Harold, you look terrific! What have you been doing?"

"Funny you should ask," Harold said, grinning ear to ear. "I met a lovely young woman at the bakery last summer, and we got married in Vegas over the Christmas holidays."

"What wonderful news, Harold!" Don exclaimed. "I'm excited for you, old buddy."

Harold had many things to say regarding the attractions of his new wife, but Don finally had to guide the conversation to his tax return.

"Well, Harold, let's see what you've got," Don said in his most businesslike manner.

As if he didn't hear him, Harold said, "Did I mention she is an amazing chef?"

"Fabulous! Now there's no excuse for not inviting me over for dinner," Don answered, glancing at his watch while reviewing Harold's files. Throughout the preparation, without pause, the bridegroom talked of his new love.

"Does your wife work?" Don inquired.

"It's working out perfectly, Don. Haven't you been listening? She's perfect!"

"Harold, it's obvious she's perfect. I just need to know if she has wages or income to enter on your tax return."

"Oh," Harold replied, somewhat red in the face. "You mean *work*, like in a job? I gotcha."

Seeing that his client was unable to concentrate on business, Don resigned himself to being a good listener and focused on Harold's interests. "Did you and your new bride go on a honeymoon?"

"Honeymoon? We're still on our honeymoon," Harold sighed.

"Somehow," Don said, "I had a feeling you were going to say that!"

TAX TRIVIA

Taxing the Rich

In 1994, the top 10 percent of taxpayers paid 57 percent of all personal income taxes collected. Those taxpayers in the top 1 percent contributed 25 percent.

And Junior Makes Four

Jon Berman, who had listed children as dependents on his latest tax return, expressed dismay when the IRS, apparently questioning his integrity, requested birth certificates for three of his children. Although he had provided their social security numbers on the return, the IRS demanded more.

"I don't understand it, Dan," Jon said to his preparer. "Why in the world would they come after me? I am an honest man."

"Let me investigate, Jon. Perhaps there's a misunderstanding," Dan said reassuringly.

After digging into the matter, Dan understood the IRS's confusion. Dan gave Jon a call to correct the mistake. "Jon," Dan said with a chuckle, "Your return states that three of your children all have the same first, middle, and last name. That's why they notified you. Obviously, it's some kind of a mistake."

"It's no mistake," Jon said. "All three times I've been married, I've had children. With each of my wives, I named my first son Jonathan Kevin Berman, after myself. So, counting me," he said with obvious pride, "there are actually four of us!"

The Little Scholar

Gerry Rosen couldn't help staring at her client's precious little five-year-old. He sat like a perfect little gentleman throughout the entire session.

When the return was completed, Gerry commented, "My goodness, you have been a good little boy."

"Thank you, ma'am," the child answered.

"Do you go to school?"

"Yes, ma'am. I'm in kindergarten."

"What do you like most about school?" Gerry asked.

"Arithmetic is my favorite subject."

"Do you know how much one and one is?"

"No, ma'am," the boy answered. "We haven't gotten that far yet."

The Outrage and Horror of Income Tax

In the early 1890s, when nearly every other major nation had such a tax, President Grover Cleveland proposed a federal income tax, in an effort to cut tariffs. His proposal was a modest 2 percent tax on all incomes over $4,000. It was branded as socialism, communism, and devilism. "If we pass this bill, free enterprise dies on the spot," predicted Senator John Sherman, father of the Sherman Antitrust Act.

Marriage Counselor: In Need Of

In a race for the best parking space at a Denver H&R Block office, a car occupied by a middle-aged man and his wife zoomed in, edging out another car. In the process, the man nearly drove his new Cadillac into the office's front window.

As a consequence, a battle ensued between the couple, witnessed by everyone in the waiting room. Arms waved, and voices rose, and car doors slammed when both husband and wife got out of their car. All eyes were upon them as they walked into the office. The receptionist greeted them, advising that there would be a fifteen-minute wait.

"You see, Frank, I told you we should have gotten here before noon," the wife said in a loud whisper. "Then there would be no waiting at all. Now let's just get out of here and come back later."

"I've had it with your demands, Liza," the man angrily shouted. "Let's just sit down and get this dang thing over with."

During their wait, the bickering continued. The waiting room occupants, finally bored by the arguing, turned their attention back to their magazines.

A tax preparer came out to the waiting room. "Frank and Liza Walden, would you please join me at my desk?"

"See, I told you it wouldn't take long," Frank said in a schoolboy "I-told-you-so" tone. "These guys have a great reputation for speedy service."

"If we had just come in earlier—" Liza started up again.

"Please come with me, Mr. and Mrs. Walden," the preparer interrupted.

The couple walked back to the preparer's desk and sat down.

"Okay," the preparer said, "what have you got for me?"

"I brought in all of our paperwork from the last—" Frank began.

"You? You brought it?" his wife cut in. "What are you talking about, Frankie? I'm the one who got it all together and made the appointment!"

"Now, now," the preparer said, "it doesn't really matter who does what. Just let me review your paperwork.

"May I ask you a few questions?" he continued.

"Yes," they said simultaneously, looking at each other in disbelief, as if it was the first time in ages they had agreed on something.

At last, we're starting to get somewhere, the preparer thought. "And what are your occupations?"

Although Frank tried to answer first, Liza won. "He's a lawyer, and I'm a marriage counselor."

The preparer didn't miss a beat. "Of course," he said. "That's just what I would have guessed."

Indiana Puts Tax on Ice

In Indiana, a sales tax was put on ice used to cool alcoholic drinks, but not on ice used to cool bottled soda.

And Babies Make Five

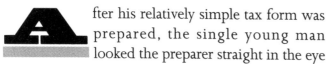fter his relatively simple tax form was prepared, the single young man looked the preparer straight in the eye and said, "Come next year, I won't have to pay a tax like this."

The tax preparer said, "Why is that, Todd?"

"Well, next year I'll have five exemptions!" he said excitedly.

"Five?" the tax preparer exclaimed.

"Yeah, I'm getting married in June, and our triplets are due in September!"

New York Popcorn Tax

New Yorkers did not pay tax on salted or buttered popcorn, but they did on caramel-coated popcorn.

Running Up the Tab

A young married couple came into an H&R Block office in Portland, Oregon, with their three-year-old son. During their ten-minute stay in the waiting room, "little Matty" wanted to play with everything. By the time tax preparer Frank Wilson came out to greet them, magazines were on the floor and several plants were ripped out of their pots.

"Matt and Terri Oberlin, I'm ready for you," Frank said, gesturing toward his desk.

"Okay, Matty, put the plant down, and let's go," his mother said in a weak voice. "All right, I guess you can bring it with you. Just don't take any more."

The receptionist, who had nurtured the plant for six months to get it to grow along the windowsill, looked on in awe.

The four of them walked over to Frank's desk and got comfortable. "Let's get started," Frank said.

The couple handed over a file, and Frank began logging their basic information into the computer. As he was typing, "little Matty" crawled under Frank's desk, and the tax preparer soon felt something pulling at his socks. "Okay, Matty, I'm sure Mommy wants to take control of you," he said. And turning to Terri, he added, "Isn't that right?"

Terri's husband looked at Frank with a baffled look on his face. "Excuse me, Frank, but just because she brings home most of the income doesn't mean—"

"No, no, no!" Frank interrupted. "I was talking about little Matty—down there. He's tugging on my feet."

Matt picked up his son and placed him on his lap. "Now you behave, young man! We're almost done."

Almost done? Frank thought. We just started.

Little Matty spotted the adding machine on the table, and began hammering at the keys, letting paper spill over the machine. His parents seemed amused.

Well, I guess that will keep him busy, Frank thought, and let out a big sigh.

"What do you do for a living?" Frank inquired.

"I'm a psychiatrist," volunteered Terri, "and Matt is looking for a new field right now."

"One of the things I was considering is training to be a tax preparer," Matt said excitedly. "How do you guys set your fees?" he asked.

With a solemn look toward little Matty, who was happily exploring the length of tape in the adding machine in an efficient hand-over-hand stripping motion, Frank quipped, "We base it on the amount of adding machine tape used in preparing the return."

You Can't Hide Your Age From Your Tax Preparer

spry pair of newlyweds came into an H&R Block office in South Carolina to get their taxes prepared. The preparer began by asking the basic questions to start a file on them.

"I'm sorry I must intrude into your personal lives, but I have to ask—how old are the two of you?"

"I'm seventy-eight years old, and my young bride is seventy-five," said the proud husband, giving his wife's hand a squeeze.

Isn't that nice, the preparer thought, falling in love again during the golden years.

"You two are very lucky," the preparer said after finishing their return.

"We know," they chimed as they stood up to leave.

"Honey, I have to use the little ladies' room," the

new bride said, with a teenagelike giggle. "I'll meet you at the car in a few minutes."

"Okay, sweetheart. In the meantime, I'll pull the car up for you."

Just seconds after the two left the preparer's desk, the woman tiptoed back in.

"Did you leave something, Mrs. Thatcher?" the preparer asked.

Suddenly shy, she said, "Well, not exactly."

A quizzical look appeared on the tax preparer's face.

Leaning over the desk, she whispered in his ear, "Please don't tell my husband, but the government better know that I'm really eighty-one years old!"

First U.S. Income Tax

The first income tax in the United States resulted from an "income duty" introduced as a temporary measure to finance the Civil War. The rates ranged from 3 to 5 percent. That tax continued until 1871, raising some $376 million in revenue—about 0.02 percent of the amount the federal government collected one hundred years later in 1971.

Do Bush Hogs Breed?

lbert Johnson, a well-known farmer from the outskirts of Mount Vernon, Ohio, came into the city to get his taxes done. Teresa Wagner, a first-year tax preparer for H&R Block, was assigned to him.

"Good morning, Mr. Johnson," she said. "I'm Teresa, and I'll be doing your return."

"You're my preparer? Well, good morning, Teresa. My, they're getting younger every year. Are you sure you can handle my taxes?" he asked. "It's a pretty big job."

Feeling a little intimidated, Teresa walked him back to her desk, trying to reassure her client. "No sweat, Mr. Johnson."

Teresa was taken aback when she opened his file labeled "Deductions." Wow, I've never seen so many deductions, she thought. I hope I'm up to this.

Johnson saw the young woman looking over his receipts. "How's it coming, Teresa?" he politely asked.

"We're making progress," she answered.

"You know how it is being a farmer these days, Teresa. It seems farming is getting more complicated every year. You can't imagine how much paperwork there is these days. Seems as though I spend more time behind my desk than I do in my fields. And the machinery is enough to break a fellow these days," he sighed.

Actually, I have no idea, she thought. A city girl, she had never heard of half of the deductions she was listing. I don't dare ask what these are, she thought, or he'll just think I'm a naive young kid.

"Yes, Mr. Johnson, that's what they say," she concurred. "I respect a farmer's work ethic and integrity. It takes a special breed to farm in today's environment. As far as I'm concerned, farming has always been the backbone of America—and it always will be."

"Well, then," he smiled, "you do know where I'm

coming from." He seemed to relax a bit more, with the knowledge that the young woman could relate to his problems.

What have I gotten myself into? she said to herself.

"And let me apologize for doubting you earlier, young lady," he said. "To look at you, I would have never imagined you knew anything about farming."

Breathing a sigh of relief, she began going through his deductions, but soon she was stumped. Bush hog? she read. This guy wants to deduct his hog?

"How long have you had your bush hog, Mr. Johnson?" She asked, anticipating Johnson would say it was accidentally listed among his deductions.

"Just bought it last fall."

"Do you plan on breeding it?" she asked.

The man gave a big belly laugh. "If I could breed farm machinery, ma'am," he said, "I'd be a millionaire."

Temporary Income Tax Becomes Permanent

With the possibility of war in Europe, Congress proposed amending the Constitution so that a temporary income tax could be enacted —and shut off when the financial emergency was over. In early 1913, two-thirds of the states had ratified the Sixteenth Amendment to the Constitution, allowing the federal government to tax "all income, from whatever source derived."

Pulling Numbers Out of the Air

ark Dawson came into an H&R Block office in San Diego to have his tax return prepared. Ben Novak, the office's veteran preparer, greeted him.

"Let's see what you've got for me," Ben said, although the man was not carrying a briefcase, folders, or even a sack.

"Well, I started to complete my return myself but I ran into a few roadblocks," Mark said, pulling an income tax form and a few wrinkled pieces of paper from his pocket.

As the two men sat at Ben's desk, he looked at the return and smiled. "I see you didn't get any further than filling in your name. I need your records so we can get started."

"Well, I don't have any records on paper, but I know all the information that you need," Mark said with contagious confidence.

"Okay, Mark, we'll give it a go."

In a joint effort, the two men started on the return, Ben asking questions and Mark supplying answers. Ben was amazed at Mark's incredible memory. How did he remember all of this information?

"Okay, Mark, we've come to your deductions. Would you like to come back later this afternoon or tomorrow with your paperwork?"

"Actually that won't be necessary," Mark answered. "I've kept good track of them in my mind. We should be just fine."

"Okay," Ben said uneasily. "How much did you spend on office supplies this year?"

Mark looked up at the ceiling for a moment. "Let's see," he said, as if he were figuring it out. "That's $940."

Shaking his head, Ben wrote the number down. "And what were your total travel expenses this year?"

Mark looked up in the air again and pulled out a figure. "Precisely $4,335," he said confidently.

"And how much for postage?"

"Let's see, that was $831.25."

It went on like this until the return was finished. "See, that wasn't so bad," Mark said. "Now how much do I owe you?"

Ben glanced up at the ceiling for a moment. "The total comes to $263.55."

"Where the heck did you get that number?" Mark asked.

Ben looked at him straight in the eye and replied, "From the same ceiling tile you used!"

Dead Women Don't File Dual Returns

Sam Milton came into the H&R Block office in Bloomington, Indiana, one snowy February morning. His tax preparer, Lisa Brooks, asked a standard question for his type of return—"Are you still married?"

"No, my wife died," the man said, delivering the sad news with a "let's-get-on-with-it" expression on his face.

"I'm really sorry to hear that, Mr. Milton," Lisa said gently. "When did she die?"

"Uh—I guess a few months ago," he said. "Yeah, about six months ago to be exact."

"Do you know the date?" Lisa asked. "So I can put it on the return?"

"Uh, I'll have to get back to you on that one. I don't remember the exact date."

That's peculiar, Lisa thought. How could he not remember when his wife died?

When she continued with his return, she noticed that Milton's wife's income listed at the same amount as the previous year. Wait a minute! Lisa thought. If she died six months ago wouldn't her salary be only half of what it was last year? Well, I'd better not get too nosy, she reminded herself.

Lisa finished Milton's return, and he thanked her and bid her farewell. Even after he left, she couldn't get her conversation with him out of her mind. Throughout the day, she kept thinking of his behavior. Between clients, she kept dwelling on why Milton didn't know the date of his wife's death. And why was her income the same amount as it was the previous year, if she had only worked six months? Something is definitely not right here, Lisa pondered.

Lisa had finally wiped all thoughts of Milton out of her mind when the telephone rang. She picked up the receiver and a woman asked, "Has Sam Milton been in today?"

"Oh, yes, ma'am, several hours ago," Lisa replied. "Is this his secretary calling?"

"No," the woman said, "this is Mrs. Milton."

"His mother?"

"No, his wife."

"Oh, you must be the new Mrs. Milton!"

"Not that new," the lady said sarcastically. "I think thirty-one years of marriage has taken the edge off the new. And what business is it of yours?"

"Well," Lisa said nervously, "I don't know how to say this, but your husband told me to put down on his return that . . . that . . . that you had died."

"Died?" She asked. Suddenly she got the picture. "No, you've got it all wrong. But I can assure you, when he gets home this evening, it will be *my husband* who will wish he was dead!"

New York Times **Predicts Gloom and Doom**

Considered a newspaper for the wealthy, the New York Times reported in an editorial on April 12, 1913, that the new 1 percent tax increase had "transferred the burdens of the many to the shoulders of the few." It predicted the new law would "tax the honest and allow the dishonest to escape." The Times said that the new tax law was so complicated that it discriminated unjustly against people who weren't good at mathematics. The newspaper pessimistically forecasted that rates were destined to double eventually to 2 percent!

Sick about Taxes?

Janet Martin had been experiencing morning sickness the entire week. If it hadn't been the middle of the tax season, she would have taken some time off. However, the office was swamped with work and Janet felt obligated to do her job.

Janet's first client of the day was Lauren Shoney, who brought what was certain to be a complicated tax return. Lauren owned several small businesses and usually claimed many deductions. She also had several tax shelters that had gone bad during the past year, and these, too, would be time-consuming to decipher.

About halfway through Lauren's return, Janet began to feel a little queasy. She continued to work on Lauren's return, even though she looked white as a ghost.

Lauren took a long look at Janet and thought, my tax lady doesn't look so good.

"Are you okay, honey?" Lauren asked.

"Yes, I'm fine," Janet said, not wanting any sympathy.

Just then, fresh coffee was being poured three desks down from where Janet and Lauren sat. At that moment, the delicious aroma seemed to Janet a nauseating stench; she quickly excused herself, making a dash to the bathroom, which was directly opposite her desk.

A few minutes later, Janet came back with a slightly red face.

"Excuse me," Janet said, embarrassed. "I'm pregnant, and I've been experiencing morning sickness lately. The whiff of that coffee really did me in."

Lauren gave a sigh of relief and sank back in her chair. "Thank God!" she exclaimed. "I thought it had something to do with those last few deductions!"

Politically Correct Coiffures

Dorothy Witkin had been coming in to the H&R Block office in Savannah, Georgia, for twelve years. Everyone in the office was familiar with her smiling face. And her southern hospitality never let her visit without bringing fresh cookies or brownies.

"Good morning, Dorothy! How have you been?" asked her tax preparer, Johnny Gordon.

"Fine, thanks, Johnny," Dorothy said. "Here, try one of these. I made oatmeal cookies this morning especially for you."

After catching up on her news for a few minutes, Johnny, licking a few crumbs from his lips, started on her return. "Looks like you did pretty well this year," Johnny said.

"Yes, I can't complain, Johnny. It was my best year ever in the catering business," she said proudly.

"All right, I'm ready to review your deductions, Dorothy. Did you bring all your check stubs and receipts this year?"

"I wouldn't forget them twice in a row," Dorothy smiled, handing him the folder.

Johnny went through her receipts and canceled checks, placing each of them in its proper category. After a dozen years of preparing her taxes, he was amazed at how little her spending habits had changed. Most of the receipts and checks were to the same places every year.

About halfway through the pile of returned checks, though, Johnny's jaw dropped. He looked up at Dorothy. The KKK! he gulped. How could she support them?

Noticing his perplexed look, Dorothy asked, "What's the matter, Johnny?"

"Nothing, Dorothy, I'm just fine," he said, flipping through her canceled checks.

He found three more checks written to the KKK.

I don't understand, he thought. How could such a sweet lady support such an organization? And the amounts are so weird—$58.25, $68.50, $43.95. She can't deduct these! What am I going to tell her?

"Um, Dorothy?"

"Yes, Johnny?" Her sweet voice seemed to belie her terrible deeds.

"You can't deduct these checks to the KKK."

"Well, I wasn't sure," Dorothy said.

"Frankly," Johnny admitted, "I'm, well, surprised. It seems so out of character."

"I know I shouldn't have," Dorothy replied, chastened. "But I have to look good on the job, so I thought I just might be able to deduct my costs at the new beauty parlor—Kathy's Kut and Kurl."

Highest Rates in U.S. History

By 1921, the first-bracket rate was increased to 4 percent on incomes over $4,000, and the top rate was 73 percent on incomes over $1 million. By 1944, the tax rate reached an all-time high, starting at 23 percent on incomes over $2,000, and 94 percent on incomes above $200,000.

A Fishy Mistake

Judy Polinsky had been with the H&R Block office in Cleveland, Ohio, for only six weeks when one of the most embarrassing moments of her life occurred. Judy, whose friends called her a "fish freak" had set up an aquarium on a stand beside her desk. In it was Wally, her favorite fish. Wally was a beautiful goldfish that had been won at the Ohio State Fair by Judy's ex-boyfriend. She had carefully held the bowl on her lap all the way from Columbus to Cleveland, and, ever since, Judy and Wally were dear friends. After a series of upgrades to larger bowls, Wally was now comfortably in his new home—a large fifteen-gallon aquarium.

Judy had brought her fair-finned friend to the office so she could watch him in between clients. "It's amazing how much stress relief Wally provides," the young tax preparer often reminded coworkers and clients.

One slow morning at the office, Judy decided to

do some "aquarium maintenance," a polite way to say "cleaning the tank." The young woman rushed through what she considered a necessary but unpleasant task. She often kiddingly said, "Wally would do the same for me if he could." Then she did three returns and began reorganizing her desk right before her lunch break. That's when Judy noticed something shiny on the floor under her desk, and it seemed to move ever so slightly. It was Wally; he was flipping—just barely. She realized she had accidentally left the protective lid off the tank. Within seconds, she placed her badly wounded friend in the tank. Between the fall and the lack of oxygen, it was too much for Wally. He swam feebly, listing to one side, and about one hour later, the poor fish made his final approach to the top.

"No, Wally, don't die on me!" she cried. "You can make it!" If her emotions could have changed matters, undoubtedly he would survived the calamity. But this was not to be Wally's fate.

Judy sat in her office for a few minutes vainly trying to calm down. When she couldn't control herself any longer, she stumbled out to the reception area to announce the terrible news to Martha, the new receptionist sent over from the temporary agency, who had just returned from her lunch.

"Wally died in the office!" Judy wailed. "I did everything I could, Martha," she sobbed, her face streaked with tears, "but I couldn't revive him!"

Judy let out a loud wail. "He's dead. Oh my God, what should we do now?" Overcome with grief, she headed to the bathroom.

The alert and resourceful receptionist assessed the situation—obviously one of Judy's clients had suffered a fatal heart attack in her office. Immediately she called 911 and placed a "closed" sign on the front door. Within minutes, a police car and an ambulance showed up at the scene. Paramedics rushed into the office with a stretcher. To their disbelief, they found one dead goldfish floating at the top of a fifteen-gallon aquarium and one slightly hysterical tax preparer.

Do I Look Dead to You?

Shouting at the top of her lungs, an elderly lady came running into an H&R Block office in Tampa, Florida. Since the office was located in a shopping mall, her commotion attracted a number of onlookers.

"What is the matter, ma'am?" Brenda, the receptionist, asked, trying to calm the nearly hysterical woman.

"Do I look dead to you? Do I look dead to you?" the worked-up lady screamed.

Brenda looked at the her in disbelief. "Noooo," she said, shaking her head.

"Well, I don't think so, either!" cried the lady.

"What makes you ask such a question?" Brenda inquired.

"I have been waiting several weeks for my check to arrive, so I finally decided to call the Social Security office," she said, a little breathless from talking so fast. "When I asked them what was taking so long, they told me that I was dead and would not receive any more checks."

"Calm down, ma'am. I am sure it is just a silly mistake that can be taken care of very easily," Brenda reassured her.

"Calm down?" cried the anxious lady. "Calm down? My landlord knows I'm not dead and he wants his money!"

After a call to the local Social Security office, Brenda discovered that it was the woman's ex-husband who, out of animosity, had falsely reported her demise.

A few phone calls later, Brenda's office was able to get the woman officially situated back into the land of the living where she belonged.

The Artificial Insemination Specialist

 young man walked into an H&R Block office in Manhattan, asking to speak to a tax preparer. The receptionist pointed to Fred Wilson at his desk. "Mr. Wilson is available, sir," she said.

After a brief introduction, Wilson asked, "What's your line of work?"

"My specialty is artificial insemination."

"What?" Wilson blurted out.

A slight grin appeared on the young man's face. "I'm an artificial insemination specialist," he reiterated more loudly. "Say, Freddy, how much do you guys charge for a simple tax return?"

This is a real wise guy, Wilson thought. Two can play at this game. I'll just go along with him.

"How much are we talking about?" the young man asked again, rubbing his index finger and thumb together.

"Our standard fee is $5,000," Wilson replied, chuckling to himself, thinking, he'll see that I have a sense of humor, too.

A serious expression appeared on the would-be client's face. He stiffened up; without saying a word, he rose to his feet and began to walk out the door.

Wilson suddenly realized that the client was on the level. Embarrassed, he called out, "Sir—"

The young man turned around and looked Wilson's way. "Are you talking to me?" he asked.

At a loss for words, Wilson mumbled, "I don't know what to say. But you see—well, to tell the truth, we don't get many artificial insemination specialists in this office."

The young man looked Wilson in the eye. "And at those prices, you'll never see me again either!"

The Pick-Up

n H&R Block office in Buffalo, New York, has a drawer at the receptionist's desk commonly referred to as the "pick-up drawer." The completed returns are kept in it, and the customers know to come there to pick up those returns.

One day a well-dressed older gentleman came into the office, and said hello in a pronounced English accent.

"Are you here for a pick-up?" the receptionist asked.

With a startled look on his face, the man replied, "My dear young lady, what kind of place is this? I simply came to get my taxes done."

Average Income Tax Rates Per Capita

In 1914, the IRS collected $3.88 for every man, woman, and child. In 1920, the per-capita figure was $50.81. During the depression, it dropped to only $12.48 per capita in 1932. In 1940, the tax per capita was $40.57; in 1950, $256.44; in 1960, $507.98; in 1970, $960.67; in 1980, $1,079.95; in 1990, $1,882.60; and in 1994, $2,479.28.

The Love Letter

William Tout came in for tax help.

"It got a little confusing, Jim," the young man informed his preparer. "I'm not familiar with a joint return."

"Don't worry, William. I've been doing your parents' return for nearly twenty-four years. Yours can't be any more complicated than theirs," he said reassuringly. "And by the way, how is Connie? You couldn't have chosen a prettier wife."

"She's doing fine, thanks."

Jim smiled at the young man. "William, what good times I used to have with your parents! It seems like just yesterday you were born—such a cute baby you were."

He stopped himself. "All right, enough talking. Let's get on with your return."

A few minutes into the return, Jim asked, "What is your wife's number?"

"Excuse me?" William said, confused.

"I can't seem to find Connie's social security number in any of this information. Do you have it?"

"Oh, her social security number. I think she said something about putting it in my lunch box this morning."

William opened his lunch box, and found a folded piece of paper, which he handed it to Jim. "I guess this is it," he said.

Jim unfolded the note, which read: "Sugar, you were simply delicious last night! Can't wait until tonight! I love you!"

On the bottom of the letter, Connie had written her social security number—in bright red lipstick.

Early Social Security Rates

When the Social Security Act became the law of the land in 1935, taxpayers' annual contributions were 1 percent of their first $3,000 in earnings, with a maximum of $30. This contribution remained the same through 1949.

It's in the Bag!

t an H&R Block office in upstate New York, a young couple with a small crying baby stopped in to drop off two large paper bags of tax information.

"Everything that you need is in these paper bags," they instructed. "Sorry it's so unorganized, but with our new baby we barely have time to do anything."

"No problem," said the tax preparer, Laura, recalling the days when her own young children were at home. "Come back this afternoon, and I should have it all squared away. Bye-bye!"

"Good luck, Laura!" Rosie, the receptionist, said, after the couple departed. "Thank goodness, I'm not a preparer."

"Hmm, this does look like more than I planned on," Laura said as she peered inside one of the bags. "It can't be that bad," she shrugged.

When Laura reached her desk, Rosie heard a loud, "Oops!" Laura had accidently knocked some of the papers on her desk to the floor.

"Let me give you a hand," Rosie volunteered, rushing back and kneeling on the floor to help.

Fifteen minutes later the two of them were still sitting on the carpet beside Laura's desk, reorganizing receipts in large piles. Getting the papers in proper order was indeed a formidable task.

"As soon as we're done," said Laura, "I'm going to take you out for a nice lunch! And don't worry about me, Rosie. If you need to visit the restroom now, go ahead, and I'll work on these stacks while you're gone."

"Excuse me," Rosie said, "but what makes you think I want to use the restroom?"

"Well, someone in here surely has gas, and it is not I!" Laura exclaimed with a chuckle.

"And I thought it was you!" Rosie mimicked her friend's sarcasm. "At least, I had the common courtesy not to say anything."

"Boy, there's an awful stench," Laura said, pointing her nose up and taking a sniff in the air. "You know, it keeps getting worse and worse."

The two started to glance around the area and suddenly Rosie pointed to the two bags. "That's it!" she exclaimed. "It's in one of those bags."

When Rosie reached into the first bag, she said, "It's filled with papers. Let's check out the other one." She rummaged deep inside the second bag, and a sick expression came over her face.

"What is it, Rosie?" Laura asked anxiously.

Rosie showed its contents to a surprised Laura. "I think your clients dropped off a sack of something that they didn't intend to give us. This one is filled with dirty diapers!"

Norway Has Highest Taxes

The country with the heaviest taxation is Norway, where the highest rate of income tax in 1992 was 65 percent—although additional personal taxes make it possible to be charged in excess of 100 percent. In January 1974, the 80 percent limit was abolished there, and some two thousand citizens were listed in the Lignings Boka as paying more than 100 percent of their taxable income. Shipping magnate Hilmar Rekstein (1897–1980) was assessed 491 percent.

A Stubborn Old Lady

recently retired woman with insufficient federal withholdings was surprised to learn she had a small balance due.

"I'm sorry, Mrs. Witkin, but you owe $160 this year," the preparer said.

"You must be doing something wrong," she shrugged. "Now go over your numbers again and figure out how much they owe me."

Although he knew he had done it correctly the first time, the preparer went through it once more for her peace of mind. "I came up with $160 again, Mrs. Witkin. The numbers are a little different now that you're retired."

Indignant that the preparer would accuse her of owing, Mrs. Witkin bellowed, "The government has been paying me to do my taxes all my life. Why in the world should it be different now that I am retired?"

TAX TRIVIA

U.S. Taxes Aren't So High After All

In 1990, the per-capita tax paid in the United States was $6,358. Other per-capita totals around the world include Canada, $8,042; Denmark, $12,235; Finland, $10,469; Germany, $8,882; Italy, $7,432; Japan, $7,432; Luxembourg, $11,516; Norway, $11,533; Sweden, $15,154; Switzerland, $10,490; Turkey, $538; United Kingdom, $6,232.

A Short Story

It was Frank Benson's first year working at H&R Block's Executive Tax Service located in a small, affluent West Coast community. Before meeting a new client, one of the most influential men in the area, Frank had been advised by his coworkers about what not to say!

"Let's just say that he's small in stature," Frank was told. "Don't make any reference to his height!"

Of course I won't, Frank thought to himself. But it would have been easier if they hadn't made such an issue out of it.

Two o'clock rolled around just as Frank was trying to finish one of his most difficult returns ever. It was also the time Jonathan Madden, the diminutive client, was scheduled to come in. Frank came out to the reception area a full fifteen minutes late.

"Please excuse my tardiness, Mr. Madden," Frank said, as he reached down to shake his client's hand.

"Forget it. Let's just get this over with," Mr. Madden said.

The two men sat down at Frank's desk and went to work on the return. Frank was extra careful throughout the interview not to make any references to the man's height.

Frank soon realized why Madden was not in such a good mood. Wow, he thought, his tax liability is more than most people's annual income.

At the end of the tense interview, Frank decided to break the ice by explaining to Madden the benefits of filing an estimated tax return. Before he could stop himself, he had blurted out, "After all, Mr. Madden, you don't want to find yourself short again next year."

Realizing his faux pas, his face flushed and he hemmed and hawed, "Ah, what I actually meant to say, is, er . . ."

To Frank's delight, Madden almost fell on the floor laughing.

Poor Howard Hughes

The highest recorded personal tax levy in the United States was $336 million, on 70 percent of the estate of Howard Hughes.

Look Who's Laughing Now

ach year H&R Block offers a tax training school, which is always a huge success. Nicole Anderson, manager at the regional office in Minneapolis, was in charge of the undercover work for the training school. That is, her job was to make sure the offices in her area were recruiting a good crop of future students. Occasionally, Nicole would pose as a prospective student to determine whether the offices were actively encouraging people to take the course and giving out the correct information.

When Nicole used the phone to spot-check the offices in her region, she always attempted to disguise her voice, so the office personnel would not recognize her. It was no easy task, however, since she was familiar to everybody. One year she decided it was time to make an extra effort to develop her disguise.

Nicole had been practicing a deep southern accent, and had also decided to give a real street address, claiming to have just moved to town. There is no way they'll know it's me this time, thought Nicole.

The first few calls went amazingly well. Nicole couldn't believe how well she pulled off her southern accent. Then came a tricky one.

"Hello, H&R Block," the receptionist at a local office answered.

"Yeah, uh, I know y'all are about to close but I was wonderin' if y'all gave, uh, tax courses?"

"We sure do," the woman answered. The receptionist then gave Nicole all of the pertinent information, asking if she wanted to sign up for the course right then.

"Could you just send me some information and let me think 'bout it, ma'am?"

"I'll be delighted," the receptionist pleasantly said.

"My name is Martha Goodard," Nicole drawled like a southern belle. "And my address is 2240 Elm Street. I wish I could give you a phone number, but I just moved in and those dang phone people are actin' purty slow."

"Did you say 2240 Elm Street?" the receptionist said in a surprised tone.

"Yeah, that's correct, ma'am, 2240 Elm Street."

"Well, I'll be darned. I guess the Johnsons did decide to move to their cabin up north. Welcome to the neighborhood, Martha! I just happen to live three houses down the street from you."

"Oh, really?" Nicole replied, her voice cracking this time. "Thanks for the information, ma'am," she croaked, hanging up the phone.

What have I done? she thought. I have to call her back and tell her who I am before she goes home. Nicole picked up the phone and hit redial.

This time an answering machine greeted her.

"Thank you for calling H&R Block, our office hours are—"

Well, I guess there is nothing I can do now, she thought. I'll just call back in the morning and let her know it was me.

The next morning, Nicole stood at her desk and picked up the phone to place a call.

"Good morning, H&R Block," said the receptionist.

"Hello, I called yesterday afternoon, and I think I talked to you about your tax course," Nicole said, already feeling a little sheepish. "Do you recall talking to a Martha Goodard?"

"It wasn't me," exclaimed the receptionist in a sad voice. "And I am sorry to say the receptionist that you spoke to was in a terrible accident after work yesterday."

"What? What do you mean? What happened?"

"Well, I really shouldn't be telling you this, but I heard she was on her way to a bakery to pick up a pie for some new neighbors on her block and—hello, are you still there?"

Nicole let out a loud gasp and felt her knees weaken. "W-would you mind repeating what you just said?" she stuttered. Before she could fully grasp what had happened, she heard a telltale roar of laughter in the background over the phone.

"Y-you set me up!" Nicole squealed. "You knew all along that it was I, didn't you?" She paused briefly and added, "Well, thank you, dear Lord!"

Five Unusual Old Ways to Pay Taxes

In ancient China, the citizens paid their taxes with large sheets of pressed tea.

The Australian natives on surrounding islands paid taxes with sharks' teeth.

The Jivara tribesmen who lived along the Amazon paid their taxes in shrunken heads.

The Ottomans imposed a tax of one son out of every five in a family. The tax boy was trained for a lifetime in the Sultan's army.

Playing cards were the first paper currency of Canada when the French governor in 1685 used them to pay some war debts. In 1765, when the Stamp Act was passed, every pack of playing cards was taxed one shilling.

The Mistaken Exhibitionist

husky man wearing the work clothes of a car mechanic dashed into an H&R Block office.

"Good afternoon, sir," Shelley McClintis greeted him.

"How you doin', ma'am? I'm Shawn Pentz, and I was wondering if you could squeeze in my return during my lunch break."

"Sure can, Mr. Pentz," Shelley answered. "I'll need to get some information from you."

A few minutes after they were seated at her desk, Shelley asked her client for his social security number.

"I know I should know it," he said, "but I have a mental blank."

"Look on your driver's license?" she suggested.

"Yes, ma'am," Shawn said, and as he got up, he began to unzip his pants.

Embarrassed, Shelley stood up quickly and said in a raised voice, "What in the world?"

"I was just—" Shawn started to say, but he was interrupted by a burly male preparer who was working at desk across from Shelley's.

"Is there a problem, Shelley?" he asked, addressing both tax preparer and red-faced client.

Again, Shawn tried to say something. "I was just trying—"

"This sort of behavior—" Shelley began.

"Will you guys just listen to me?" Shawn finally shouted. "My driver's license is in my slacks underneath my work clothes. I was just trying to get to it!"

He then pulled his work pants down to reveal a second pair of pants with his wallet in the front pocket. "Here it is," the man said angrily. "Now I think an apology is in order."

Shelley and her male coworker were dumbfounded. Certainly an apology was in order.

"I am terribly sorry, sir," her coworker said. "But working in this part of town, and, you know, all kinds of people coming in here—"

"And please forgive me, Mr. Pentz," Shelley added sincerely.

"No problem, guys, no harm done," Shawn said, breaking into laughter as he zipped up his work pants.

Shawn's return was completed free of charge!

TAX TRIVIA

Itemized Returns

In 1988, only 29.2 percent of returns filed were itemized.

H&R Block Delivers!

It was nearing the April 15 deadline when an obviously pregnant woman dropped into a chair in the reception area of an H&R Block office in Las Vegas. During her five-minute wait, the woman was obviously uncomfortable. She fidgeted and squirmed from side to side in her chair.

"Is there anything I can do for you, ma'am?" the receptionist asked. "Would you like a glass of water?"

"Yes," the woman answered. "And while we're on the subject of water, just make sure somebody does my return before my water breaks."

"I'll have the next available tax preparer see you, ma'am," the receptionist replied.

Just then, Ron Baxter came to the waiting room and introduced himself.

"Glad to meet you—oooooooh—I'm Ruthie Shapiro, and, yes, I am pregnant, and, yes, I'm going to have my baby any minute!"

"Let's scoot on back to my desk, and we'll do this as quickly as possible, ma'am." Ron said.

Halfway through the return Ruthie's discomfort increased. "Oh, boy, I'm getting those sharp pains!"

CONGRATULATIONS! IT's an Additional Standard Deduction.

she exclaimed, grasping her stomach and beginning to lean against the back of her chair.

"Why don't we call for an ambulance?" a nervous Ron suggested.

"Only if you follow me to the hospital and finish my return when the baby is born."

"Excuse me?" Ron said, his voice suddenly weak.

"That's right, this is the last day I'll be able to have my return prepared. I don't want to file it late."

"But, but—" Ron sputtered.

"No buts!" the woman said. "Can't you see, I'm going to have my baby any minute now."

Ron grabbed the phone. He dialed 911, his voice quavering as he gave instructions.

"Just hang on until they get here, and I promise I'll finish the return at the hospital once you have the baby."

"Oh, no! I think my water just broke," Ruthie said, grabbing Ron's arm as she lay down on her side on the carpet.

"Just hold on a few more minutes!" Ron begged hoarsely, bending over her. "They're almost here!"

At this point, the entire office was alerted. Fortunately, one of the clients in the waiting room was an emergency medical technician, who heroically delivered the baby on the office floor minutes before the ambulance arrived.

TAX TRIVIA

Your Share of the National Debt

By the end of 1992, it was estimated that the United States' total outstanding debt—including government, business, and consumers—reached $10.6 trillion, up from $3.9 trillion in 1980. In 1980, the outstanding debt was only $17,116 per person, compared to $42,277 by the end of 1991.

The Bonus

fter reviewing Mitchell Marks's papers, his tax preparer asked, "What's this hundred-dollar bonus?"

"Oh, that's the reward I was paid for the suggestion I gave the company. It was chosen as the best money-saving idea for the month of August."

"What was your suggestion?"

"I told the company they ought to reduce the reward from $200 to $100," Marks said with a wide grin.

TAX TRIVIA

Tax Advantage for Small–Busted Women!

A law is on the books in England that exempts women with bust measurements of less than thirty-two inches from paying the standard 10 percent sales tax on dresses.

The Deli Owner

fter fifteen years with H&R Block in Manhattan, Ben Segal thought he had seen everything. But when he looked at his client, Sammy Weinberg, sitting across the desk from him, Ben couldn't stop a big grin from stealing across his face.

"Sammy," Ben said, "you own a successful delicatessen in the Bronx, and you live like a king. So how can you claim your business netted you only $8,000 last year?"

"Yeah, well, it was a bad year, Ben."

"A bad year?" Ben exclaimed. "You took a trip to Miami Beach, and another to the Caribbean."

"True enough."

"The IRS isn't stupid, Sammy. First, you're claiming them as business trips. Come on! Second, they're gonna want to know how a deli owner making eight grand is able to take his wife on two nice trips in the same year. You're asking for an audit, Sammy. Now tell me—how are you going to explain yourself?"

After a brief pause, he said brightly, "We deliver?"

TAX TRIVIA

Withholding Tax Act of 1943

In an effort to bring in more tax money for the war effort, the *Withholding Tax Act* was passed. It took pressure off domestic prices by reducing the take-home pay of wage earners. In the long run it has eased the pain of paying stiff income taxes for honest taxpayers and has helped foil dishonest ones who try to avoid paying their taxes.

Swollen Feet

young man wearing a dirty, damp white apron walked into an H&R Block office in Pittsburgh. The receptionist advised him to expect a fifteen-minute wait.

"If there's any way to speed it up, I'd be most appreciative, ma'am," the man said. "I'm on a break from work, and the dishes are piling up."

Shortly afterward, Rob Peterson came over to invite the anxious man to his desk.

The dishwasher got right to the point. "Someone has told me it is possible to deduct work clothes. Is that true, Mr. Peterson?"

"It is true, but only under certain circumstances," Rob said.

"Well, I just bought this $120 pair of steel-toed boots for work," the young man said.

"You don't work in construction, do you?"

"No, I'm a dishwasher down at the Mexican joint on Liberty."

"I'm sorry but I can't put steel-toed boots down as a deduction for a dishwasher. If you worked on a construction crew, the circumstances might be different," the tax preparer said.

"I'm afraid you don't understand what it takes to be a dishwasher," the man said warily. "If you'd dropped as many pots and pans on your feet as I have, you'd surely understand why I need steel-toed boots."

"I'm sorry, but the tax code says that work clothes are deductible only if they can be worn only on that job. That is, they cannot be worn on the street. Understand?"

"What do you mean?" the dishwasher asked, looking at his watch with a sigh.

"Well, let me give you an example. Liberace once tried to fight it out with the IRS, and they told him, 'We're sorry, Liberace, but your clothes can also be worn on the street.' As the story goes, Liberace brought in one of his outfits, and asked, 'Would you wear these clothes on the street?' And he got the deduction. Do you see what I'm getting at, sir?"

Without a moment of hesitation, the dishwasher ripped off his boots and socks, and put his black and blue feet on Rob's desk. "Did Liberace's feet look like these?"

Rob took one glance at the man's swollen feet and put down the cost of the steel-toed boots as business expense.

Official Manual of IRS

Hailed as the world's most confusing publication, the official manual of the Internal Revenue Service is an agglomeration of 38,000 pages.

It's a Guesstimate!

The elderly man handed a return he had previously prepared to H&R Block tax preparer Aaron Woodruff.

A puzzled look appeared on Aaron's face. He couldn't help wondering why Tom Berk was handing him a completed form. After all, that was his job.

The tax preparer glanced at the return and shook his head. He was obviously puzzled. What was his long-time client up to? he pondered.

"Er, Tom, you completed this return without filling in your name . . ."

"I did that on purpose," Tom replied.

"Why on earth?" Aaron asked.

"It's a guesstimate," the man answered with a grin. "Let's let the Internal Revenue Service guess who I am!"

TAX TRIVIA

Big Businesses Have Big Returns

The 1995 annual tax return for Chrysler Corporation stood six feet high and was prepared by a staff of fifty-five.

Top Ten Witty Quotations

Everybody has something to say about taxes. The following are the authors' ten favorite quotations:

"The income tax has made more liars out of the American people than golf has."

—Will Rogers

"Blessed are the young, for they shall inherit the national debt."

—Herbert Hoover

"The taxpayer—that's someone who works for the federal government but doesn't have to take a civil service examination."

—Ronald Reagan

"Behind every successful man is the IRS."

—Anonymous

"The average taxpayer may be America's first national resource to be exhausted."

—Anonymous

"What is the difference between a taxidermist and a tax collector? The taxidermist takes only your skin."

—Mark Twain

"The way taxes are, you may as well marry for love."

—Joe E. Lewis

"Milk the cow, but do not pull off the udder."

—Greek proverb

"The hardest thing in the world to understand is the income tax."

—Albert Einstein

"Today it takes more brains and effort to make out the income-tax form than it does to make the income."

—Alfred E. Neuman

A Tough Habit to Kick

I'm sorry to hear that!" Eddie Simpson said. "You mean you sincerely told her you'd quit gambling and she still wants a divorce?"

"Yes. Even though I've been going to Gamblers Anonymous twice a week, she still won't budge one iota. Elaine insists the problem won't go away. What can I possibly do?" Tim asked, his voice a sad monotone.

"Well," Eddie said, while flipping through Tim's return, "I guess you gotta keep trying. Why don't the two of you take a little vacation with your refund?"

"Refund?" Tim asked, obviously surprised.

"That's correct," Eddie answered. "$777 on the nose."

Wide-eyed, Tim looked up in amazement. "Did you say right on the nose? Are you telling me it's exactly seven-seven-seven. Three sevens?"

"Yes, Tim. What's the big deal?"

"The number," Tim said, with sudden excitement. "Why, do you know the odds of getting a refund with that number?"

"Yeah, I guess it is kind of unusual," Eddie said.

"Unusual? It's ironic! It's—it's—amazing!" Tim said. "Well, I'm out of here. I've got something very important I must do."

"Like what?" Eddie asked.

"The number seven is going to make me a rich man at the racetrack this afternoon!"

Watch Your Language, Ma'am!

 middle-aged woman nervously paced back and forth while waiting her turn at an H&R Block office in Los Angeles, California.

"Just take a seat, ma'am," the receptionist said. "Somebody will be with you in about fifteen minutes."

"Fifteen minutes! What kind of an operation is this?" the woman bellowed as she took a seat.

"What a bunch of %$*&*@!" she mumbled under her breath.

Others in the waiting room glanced over their magazines at the sputtering lady.

Gary Price, who happened to be one of the office's most conservative preparers, came out to the waiting room a few minutes later.

"Meredith Johnson, I'm ready to see you," he announced.

"It's about time. I've been dying in this @%$#*!" she said. Meredith grabbed her purse, cursing and stomped across the room.

Persevering through the woman's numerous expletives, Gary asked her what her occupation was.

"Author," she replied flatly.

"Exactly what type of books do you write, ma'am?" he asked.

"Children's Christian books," she answered.

Having an Eye on Taxes

n eighty-two-year-old H&R Block client had an embarrassing thing happen to him.

When his preparer, Janet Wallace, pointed out his large balance due, the elderly gentleman leaned over the table to have a good look at what he believed was an outrageous number, whereupon his glass eye popped out and bounced across the table, bounding into Janet's lap!

His concern over his balance momentarily forgotten, he began laughing. And after the stalwart Janet recovered from her initial shock, she had a chuckle too. After all, taxes are a serious business, well worth keeping an eye on.

Too Charitable

argaret Johnson stormed into an H&R Block office in Little Rock, Arkansas, bursting with excitement. She was talking so fast, even her long-time preparer, Ted Simmons, couldn't understand her.

"Calm down, Margaret!" Ted said. "I can't make out a word you're saying!"

"You mean you didn't hear about it on the news?" she panted.

"Hear what news?"

"About the $200,000 I won in the lottery last week!"

"That's wonderful, Margaret!" he exclaimed. "No, I hadn't heard about your good fortune. Congratulations!"

After thinking about how he'd feel about winning a lottery and what he'd do with the booty, he asked, "So, what do you plan to do with your winnings?"

She corrected him, "You mean what did I already do with my money! Well, I paid off some debts, gave my two kids money to use as down payments on new homes, and bought that beautiful brand-new Cadillac out there!" she said, proudly pointing to the parking lot. Ted leaned around the corner to glance out the storefront window at the spanking-new, cream-colored Seville outside.

"Wow, it sure is a beauty," he sighed.

"The rest, of course, went to the church. After all, I wouldn't have won it without the good Lord behind me."

"Uh, Margaret, you do know you have to pay taxes on your winnings—don't you?" he questioned.

Margaret's excited expression turned into a blank stare. "Oh? Well, it can't be much, can it?"

After penciling a few figures on his desk pad, he asked, "Well, do you consider $42,000 much money?"

The suddenly crestfallen Margaret's blue eyes brimmed with tears. "Oh, Ted, what am I going to do? I don't have $42,000! All I have left is $5,000 that I was going to use to redo my kitchen. I couldn't even sell my new car to raise the $42,000!"

"Well"—Ted grasped for something positive to say—"maybe the good Lord will give you some money back!"

The church did, in fact, pay for the taxes on her winnings.

TAX TRIVIA

A Lot of Words

One sentence in a tax instruction used by a high percentage of small-business owners in the United States consists of 436 words— compared to only 266 words in the Gettysburg Address!

Birth Control Pills

It was late in the day, and H&R Block tax preparer Barbara Criswell was just finishing her review of allowable deductions on Gretchen and Andrew Lowell's return. It was the newlyweds' first time to file a joint return, and Barbara sensed the young couple was actually enjoying the "togetherness" of what millions consider an annoying chore.

Out of nowhere, a serious expression appeared on the pretty bride's face. "Speaking of medical expenses, can I deduct my birth control pills?" she asked.

"Yes, prescription drugs can be deducted," Barbara answered with a slight smile, "but when birth control pills don't work, you get an even bigger tax break!"

Just Look It Up in the Tax Code!

There are 1,378 pages in the IRS tax code, which is divided into 1,563 sections. Its companion, Federal Tax Regulations for 1994, contains an additional 6,500 pages.

Tom and Jerry

Frank Montrose, a well-dressed, middle-aged man, came in to get his tax return prepared just before closing time. Tax preparer Rick Spencer walked his client back to his desk and after a few minutes of small talk got down to business.

Two grueling hours later, after sorting through Frank's information, Rick asked Frank if he had any exemptions.

"Yes, nine," replied Frank.

"Nine exemptions?" Rick said, a little surprised.

"That's correct," Frank said uneasily. "I have nine beautiful kids: Rusty, Donna, Margaret, Craig, Ed, Lisa, Dave, Tom, and Jerry."

"Tom and Jerry?" Rick echoed. He was feeling a little giddy after his long day. "Who is that—your cat and mouse?"

The man didn't crack a smile, which made Rick feel suddenly uneasy.

"Look, I'm terribly sorry," Rick said hastily. "I didn't mean to be flip. It's just been a very long day. I didn't mean anything by it."

"No apology necessary," Frank said. "I was just surprised you figured it out. Tom is my dog and Jerry happens to be my cat! I've been claiming them for years."

Nondeductible Drugs

s a public service, each year H&R Block tax preparers visit college campuses across the country to conduct student workshops. Not only is this practice informative to the students, it also attracts future clients for H&R Block.

A few days after such a talk at the University of Colorado, a young student came into the local H&R Block office to get his tax return prepared.

"I'd do it on my own," he told preparer Shirley Arnold, "but I'm not sure how to deduct the drugs I use."

"What exactly do you mean?" Shirley asked.

"Well, I heard one of your people speak at my dormitory last week, and he said that under certain conditions, drugs are deductible as a medical expense."

"Yes, that is correct in certain circumstances," Shirley said, cautiously peering over her reading glasses. "What kind of drugs are you planning to deduct?"

"Well, I don't have any receipts or anything, but I have spent quite a bit on marijuana and other drugs," he informed her.

She looked closely at him, and he appeared quite serious. "Is there any way I can deduct these expenses?" he continued.

"Well, I think you must be kidding me," she replied. "Surely you realize that the IRS code applies only to prescription drugs!"

"Well, I wasn't sure," the student said philosophically, "but considering the amount of money I stood to save, I knew I'd be a fool not to ask."

Questionable Marital Status

Several years back, it was a company procedure for the front-desk receptionist to obtain all the standard information from clients before they met with their preparers. And with good reason, a number of male clients were smitten with Verna, a particularly attractive H&R Block secretary in Santa Barbara, California.

One question Verna asked before sending clients to an assigned tax preparer was, "What is your marital status?" In reaction to Verna's striking beauty, some married men had been known to claim bachelorhood.

Chuck Knowles was no exception. Although he was "happily married," he just couldn't bring himself to tell the truth when Verna asked the question.

An hour after he had left the H&R Block office (filing as a single taxpayer), his wife happened to call there looking for him. She wanted to ask Chuck to stop by the convenience store for some milk on his way home.

"I'm sorry," Verna said. "Coincidentally, we did have a man by that name here today, but I'm sure he's not the Charles Knowles you're looking for. Our Chuck Knowles was single."

"What?" asked the stunned Mrs. Knowles. "It sounds like there is some mistake."

After putting down the receiver, Mrs. Knowles decided it would be prudent for her to pay a visit to the H&R Block office to investigate how a mistake of this nature could have happened.

One look at the exquisite receptionist was all she needed to figure out what was wrong with their tax return. It was as plain as day—Chuck was in serious trouble!

Friends May Forsake You

fter listening to her client's hard-luck story, Lois Brown sympathized. "I'm sorry to hear you've had such terrible financial difficulties since I did your return last year," she said.

"It happens," Sid Black answered philosophically. "But the worst part is, since I lost my money, half my friends don't know me anymore."

In an effort to cheer him, she asked brightly, "But what about the other half?"

Black shrugged his shoulders and replied, "They don't know I lost it yet."

Average Time to Prepare Taxes

The IRS estimates that the average American family spends 27 hours to keep records and prepare an itemized Form 1040 with a few additional schedules. The average Form 1040 without any schedules takes 11 hours, 35 minutes to complete. The Schedule C (business income) averages 10 hours, 16 minutes.

Getting Around

proud young father sat down at Rita Wayland's desk, brimming with excitement. "I have two newborn baby girls to claim for last year, Mrs. Wayland."

"That's wonderful," she said. "How exciting to have twins!"

"Well, they're not exactly twins," he said. "One was born March 2, and the other was born April 5."

Rita didn't mean to stare at the man with a bewildered look on her face, but she did. "How could that be?" she questioned.

He shrugged and smiled. "They have different mamas."

Highest-Taxed Residents

The citizens of the following states paid the highest taxes per resident in fiscal 1994:

State	Cost per resident
Connecticut	$7,105
New Jersey	6,680
Alaska	5,839
Massachusetts	5,760
Delaware	5,733
New York	5,714
Maryland	5,485
Illinois	5,415
New Hampshire	5,202
Washington	5,102

Don't Judge a Book by Its Cover!

At the end of a long day during tax season, Tom and Liza, the last two preparers in the office, flipped a coin to decide which of the last two walk-in clients of the day each would handle. One man in a business suit carried a thick briefcase; and the other, obviously a working man, carried a lunch pail. Since both Tom and Liza were anxious to call it a day, each wanted to prepare the working man's return.

"I'll take heads," Tom said, as Liza flipped the coin.

"You lose!" Liza announced with a wide grin.

Tom invited his well-dressed client to his desk. The man turned out to be a third-grade teacher who had stopped only to ask a few questions about his return on his way home for the evening. His briefcase was filled with his students' homework papers.

That was not the case with Liza's client. The working man was a highly successful general contractor with three cardboard boxes full of papers in his truck waiting to be organized. Four hours into the return, Liza had to ask the man to come back the next day to finish up.

"That'll be no problem, Liza," the man said graciously. "But if it's okay with you, I won't be able to come in until after-hours again."

Pay That with a Smile, Partner

r. Phil Bullock complained to his longtime H&R Block tax preparer about his tax liability that was due.

"Now, Phil, pay your taxes with a smile," his friend told him jokingly.

"I would love to," Mr. Bullock said sarcastically, "but it's my understanding they insist on cash!"

Taxing (Soaking) the Rich

Rich Americans do pay their share—and then some. In 1992, there were 3.8 million returns filed with adjusted gross incomes exceeding $100,000; these represented 3.3 percent of the 115.4 million filed, and they had a federal income tax liability of $197.4 billion. The amount that the people in this 3.3 percent group paid was 39.2 percent of the total $503.9 billion tax liability due.

Cruisin'

The owner of a successful insurance firm came in to have his taxes prepared during the heart of tax season. After viewing the owner's lengthy list of deductions, the preparer asked if there were any other deductions he wanted to add.

"Oh, I almost forgot. I took every one of my employees on a six-day cruise through the Caribbean for Christmas. The total bill came out to over $50,000!"

"Fifty grand?" said the astonished preparer. "Just how many people actually work for you?"

The man chuckled. "Oh, I'd say about two-thirds."

Even Little Taxes Add up for the Rich

The Medicare tax of 1.45 percent had its cap removed in 1994. Back then, a taxpayer stopped paying 1.45 percent after the first $135,000 of income, but now it is calculated on total earned income. This includes bonuses and exercised stock options.

This may not mean much to the average taxpayer, but it did to, say, Disney's CEO, Michael Eisner. In 1994, Eisner received nearly $11 million (including salary, bonus, and restricted stock). As a result, instead of paying a Medicare tax of $1,957 (1.45 percent of $135,000), he got hit with $159,500.

Do You Take Tips?

Halfway through his return, an elderly man with four grocery sacks full of unorganized papers asked his preparer, "Is tipping permissible for H&R Block tax preparers?"

The exhausted young preparer looked the man in the eye and said, tongue-in-cheek, "No, sir, but if they asked if you gave me one, I'd lie like anything to save you."

Where Our Tax Dollars Go (by percent)

According to the Tax Foundation, here's where our tax dollars went in 1994 versus 1984:

	1984	1994
Transportation	3	2
Education	3	3
Veterans' Benefits	3	3
Income Security	13	14
Debt Interest	13	14
Health	10	17
Defense	27	19
Social Security	20	21
Other	8	7

All My Children

 weather-beaten, elderly woman came into an H&R Block office in a small town in Alabama to get help with her taxes.

"My old man use to take care of all that tax stuff but he gone off and died on me last month. Can y'all help me?"

"Surely, ma'am," said a sympathetic preparer, as he guided her to his desk.

"Do you have any children?" the preparer asked.

"You bet I do," the woman yelled out as she nodded her head. "Let me see, there's Vera Evelyn, and Ida Novene, Robert Carl and Bernice Eugenia, and Arthur Bryan and—"

"Sorry for interrupting you ma'am, but if you could just give me the number—"

"Number!" she exclaimed indignantly. "We ain't got around to numbering 'em yet. We ain't run out of names!"

TAX TRIVIA

A 1 Percent Tax—Who Cares!

A 1913 income-tax law provided for a normal tax of 1 percent on incomes of $3,000 to $20,000 (the starting point was $4,000 for a married taxpayer), with a modest surtax above that level. The highest surtax was 6 percent on incomes over $500,000. There was also a 1 percent tax on corporate income. Since most citizens in 1913 had incomes below $4,000, Americans accepted it without worry.

The Southpaw

Looking over Fred Simpson's ledger, Sean Hamilton was having trouble making heads or tails of it. He finally figured out the problem. "It seems you entered all the debit items under credit," he announced.

Leaning across the desk, Simpson said, "Let me take a look."

"See, right here," the tax preparer explained, pointing to his client's work papers.

"Oh, that's because I'm left-handed."

TAX TRIVIA

The High Costs of Taxation

In 1995, prior to April 15, an estimated $40 billion to $200 billion was spent in direct costs of tax compliance in the United States. There were also $7.6 billion in costs to the IRS.

The Hothead

hile accompanying client Ed Ellsworth to the IRS office, preparer Steve Cunningham was asked, "What's the name of the agent we're meeting with?"

"Richard Maxwell."

"Maxwell? Why that's the same rotten no-good guy I had last year when I did my own return."

"No kidding," Cunningham replied.

After a slight pause, Ellsworth said, "You know, I feel like I'd like to punch Maxwell in the nose again."

"Again?" Cunningham said in astonishment.

"Yeah, and I felt the same way last year."

The Receptionist

 well-dressed man walked into a Boston H&R Block office, asking to speak to the office manager.

"Who shall I say is calling?" Sally asked.

"The name is Clinton Stillman."

"What is the nature of your business?" Sally inquired.

"Well, let's just say I'm a salesman, a bill collector, and a personal friend."

"Oh, in that case, he's out of town, he's with a client, and you'll find him at the second door on the right."

TAX TRIVIA

Vanishing Exemptions

In 1954, the average American family's exemptions amounted to 57 percent of its income—but today, only 25 percent.

The Check is in the Mail, in the Mail . . .

H & R Block tax preparer Lois Nelson sat with her client, Fred Boswell, across the desk from Internal Revenue Service agent Neil Walters.

"Mr. Walters," Boswell asked, "did the IRS get the check I mailed?"

"Better than that," Walters answered. "We got it twice—once from you and once from the bank."

TAX TRIVIA

Least Taxed

The sovereign countries with the lowest income tax in the world are Bahrain and Qatar. No matter what one's income is, it is not taxable! It's nice to have all that oil in the ground, isn't it?

Who Was That Blonde?

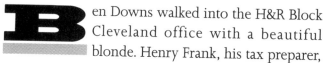

en Downs walked into the H&R Block Cleveland office with a beautiful blonde. Henry Frank, his tax preparer, was puzzled, remembering that Downs was usually accompanied by his decidedly brunette wife.

"Good morning," Frank greeted Downs. "It's good to see you."

"Same here," Downs said.

"Say, where's the women's room?" the blonde asked.

"Right over there," Frank answered, pointing to a door across the room.

"Be back in a flash, honey."

Now she's calling him honey, Frank thought, aghast.

"Say, Ben," Frank asked, "I'm embarrassed to ask . . ."

"Ask what?"

"Who's the blonde?"

Downs laughed. "She's the brunette I was with last year!"

Estate Tax Returns

During 1994, the IRS audited 15 percent of the 73,000 estate tax returns that were filed in 1993. This compared to the 17 percent for the previous year. In 1989, 24 percent of the nation's estate tax returns were audited.

Although the percentage of audited estate tax returns has dropped, in 1994, the total amount of added tax and penalties colllected by the IRS was $1.25 billion as compared to $1.05 billion in 1993. In 1994, the audit rate for estates valued at $5 million and over was 48 percent. Estates valued between $1 million and $5 million were audited at a rate of 23 percent, and estates valued at less than $21 million had an audit rate of 8 percent.

Sorry, Wrong Number

ne H&R Block office has a very similar phone number to the Blockbuster Video in the area. Half a dozen times a day, the tax office gets calls really intended for Blockbuster. They go something like this:

"Do you have *Grumpy Old Men*?" asked one caller.

"Only during tax season, sir," insisted the witty receptionist.

"Is *The Wizard* in?" asked another caller.

"Speaking," replied a weary tax preparer.

"I'm interested in *The Way We Were*, someone else inquired.

"Who isn't?" another wise guy answered.

And then there's the caller who asked for *A Fist Full of Dollars*.

"Ah, you must mean a refund," the tax preparer said.

Surprisingly, some of the calls bring in new business.

"Hello, H&R Block," the receptionist answered the phone.

"This isn't Blockbuster Video?" asked one caller.

"No, it's H&R Block, the tax preparers."

"Thanks for reminding me!" said the alarmed caller. "I haven't filed my return yet. Can I make an appointment?"

Good News

client called his H&R Block tax preparer, Fran Green. "Did you hear the good news, Fran?"

"What good news is that?" she asked.

"They're closing down the IRS."

"Excuse me?"

"You heard me, they're closing down the IRS!" he assured her. "The letter I received today said 'Final Notice.'"

IRS Workers

At present, there are 114,000 employees of the Internal Revenue Service. This figure does not include an even larger number of Americans who work as private accountants, tax lawyers, bookkeepers, etc.

And Baby Makes Three

In getting to know her new clients, tax preparer Linda Parker innocently asked, "Do you have any children?"

"Our son will be two months old next week, on the second of April," Patti Ferguson proudly announced.

"Yes, ma'am, we have a little Dennis Jr.," Dennis Sr. said.

"That's wonderful," Linda said. "You'll be able to list him as a dependent come next April."

"Right on," Dennis responded.

Getting back to business, the tax preparer inquired, "Are you planning to file jointly or separately for last year?"

"Do we have a choice?" Patti asked.

"Of course."

"Actually, I don't think we do," Dennis said.

"Sure you do," the preparer assured him.

"You don't understand," he commented. "We weren't married last year."

"Oh, I could have sworn . . ." She blushed. "Yeah, I guess I was thinking . . ."

"We just got married this past January," Patti volunteered.

"It's the baby that threw you off," Dennis said.

"They say this often happens in the case of a first child, but never afterward," Linda smiled.

Phony Social Security Cards

The IRS was stumped a few years back when it received hundreds of income tax returns all bearing the same social security number. It turned out that a leather-goods company had come out with a new, popular wallet that year, and for demonstration purposes, the company had inserted a facsimile of a social security card into the slot of each wallet.

Nobody could have predicted the owners of the new wallets would assume they were supposed to use the new social security cards!

American Averages

In a lifetime, the average American files 42 income tax returns. The average American spends 464 hours preparing those forms. The average American earns $1,235,720 in his lifetime, and of this sum pays $178,364 in taxes.

Odds of Being Audited

*In 1981, the odds of an individual being audited were 1 in 56. In 1992, these odds dropped to 1 in 110 and remained at about 0.8 or 0.9 percent for three years. However, with five thousand new IRS "enforcement" employees hired in late 1994, the odds were 1 in 50 in 1995 that the average American taxpayer would be audited.

*The IRS extracts $5,330 out of the average taxpayer who gets audited.

*An estimated 2.4 percent of corporate returns are audited; 1.4 percent of all partnerships; but for sole proprietorships with gross revenues in excess of $100,000 the rate increases to 5.4 percent.

*A Las Vegas resident has a five times greater chance of being audited than a Providence, Rhode Island, resident.

*Manhattan residents are about 70 percent more likely to be audited than are Chicago residents.

*The greatest odds of being audited in a particular state are in the state of Washington, where the risk is almost double that of Maine, the lowest state. This is true because residents of Washington, like other western states, tend to more often be self-employed and involved in cash businesses.

Unwarranted Exhaustion?

After a grueling twelve-hour day at the office during the heart of tax season, preparer Colleen Grant came home and melted into her couch. Her seven-year-old daughter, who had just come into the living room from playing outdoors, asked her wilted mom what was wrong.

"I've been at work all day," her mom told her. "I'm exhausted!"

"How can you possibly be so tired?" the child asked. "All you do at work is sit at your desk and play on the computer!"

Acting Busy

During Tom Jones's first week of employment at the H&R Block in Grand Junction, Colorado, business was very slow. Compared to the fast pace of his hometown, Los Angeles, slow-moving Grand Junction was quite a culture shock to the usually hard-working young tax preparer.

During his first few days at work, he must have rearranged his file folders a dozen times just to keep busy.

Suddenly he noticed that his office manager was about to walk past his desk. Panic-stricken, he thought, I can't let her see me just sitting here!

Hastily, he sat up straight, picked up the telephone receiver, and in his busiest, most efficient tone, said, "Yes, Mr. Johnson, I'll have your tax return done by the end of the week. . . . Very well, I'll call you later. Good-bye." He officiously hung up the phone and raised his glance to greet his boss, who had stopped and was standing over his desk.

"Oh," he said to her, anxious to keep up the charade. "I didn't see you. Sorry to keep you waiting."

"No, problem, Tom," the office manager said with a chuckle. "I just thought I'd stop by to let you know that your phone will be connected first thing in the morning."

Marrying for Money

limo pulled up in front of an H&R Block office in Portland, Maine, late in the evening on April 7. When a newly married couple exited from the back door, it certainly caught everyone's attention. The driver, carrying the long train of the wedding gown, followed the two into the reception area and took a seat beside them.

"Good evening," said Beverly, the receptionist. "And congratulations! Now, unfortunately, it's past our closing time, but it would be no problem to schedule you in the morning."

"No, no, no," the groom said. "We got married today and rushed in here so we could file our return before

we leave on a two-week honeymoon in the Far East. If we can't get it done today, we'll miss the April 15 deadline!"

Richard Jones, the firm's veteran preparer, happened to be listening. "Why, what are you talking about, Bev? Surely you got my memo this morning about H&R Block's newest rule. Anyone that walks into our office in wedding garb gets immediate service. Remember?"

The bride and groom broke into big smiles.

"Have a seat at my desk," Richard said. "We'll have you out of here in no time!"

"Oh, yes," Bev smiled. "That memo!"

Working on Commission

In 1903, IRS employees were paid a commission that was based on tax collections. Back then the commissioner's annual earnings were $6,000. Since then, tax collections have increased by 5,000 percent. No wonder IRS chief Richardson has joked that it would be a good idea today to be paid by commission!

The Accrual Bookkeeper

Jennifer Fowles, a successful restaurant owner in Seattle, Washington, dashed into her local H&R Block office. This wasn't the first time she had come in with a load of paperwork.

"Good morning, Jennifer. Say, what's the problem?" asked Julie Spear.

Jennifer looked into her eyes. "Julie, how long have you been preparing my returns?"

"It must be ten years now," Julie said.

"And how many times have I come in with my books in order?"

"I can't ever remember them being incredibly organized, but that never stopped us from doing your return," Julie said. "What makes you ask?"

"It's just that I can never seem to get a bookkeeper who does a decent job. I've been through five or six since the restaurant opened. The one I have now is—hands down—the worst! I don't even think she knows how to add or subtract."

Trying to be helpful, Julie decided to ask which method of bookkeeping the bookkeeper used. "Does she use accrual method?"

After a short silence, Jennifer looked up and said, "Well, she isn't exactly cruel, but she's not what you'd call kind either."

A Case of Hiccups

H&R Block's Frank Richmond had just put down a half-filled glass of ice water, when his long-time client Steve Bennett rushed into the office and asked, "What's the quickest way to stop hiccups?"

Responding to the emergency, the helpful Frank dashed the water on Bennett's face.

"What the heck did you do that for?" his soaked client sputtered.

"It worked, didn't it? It stopped your hiccups."

"It's not me," Bennett said. "My wife's in the car and *she* has the hiccups!"

The Shoe Box
Full of Horrors

ne early afternoon a young man carrying a shoe box walked into an Oklahoma City H&R Block office to have his taxes prepared.

John, the tax preparer closest to the front door, remembered the last guy that had walked in with a shoe box. It took nearly four hours to get his mixed-up hodgepodge of receipts straightened out. John looked at his watch and thought, "I guess I won't make it to my son's basketball game after all."

Cynthia, at the desk next to John's, saw the shoe box too. "May I help you?" she asked the shoe box man.

"Yes, I need a little help with my taxes. Is there anyone available?"

"I'd be delighted to help you, sir. Please, make yourself comfortable while I make a quick phone call."

Cynthia dialed a number, tapped her fingers on the desk while waiting for an answer, and finally whispered, "Honey, do you mind sending out for pizza for the kids tonight?" Looks like I'll be here overtime." There was a brief pause, and she said, "Thanks, Sweetie. See you in a few hours."

"Are you ready for me now?" the man asked.

"Yes, sir," Cynthia said. "Let's see what you have in your shoe box."

"Never mind those," the man said. "I just picked up a new pair of tennis shoes for the spring league that's about to start." He then handed Cynthia a slim folder of neatly organized paperwork. It was one of her quickest returns ever, and she made it home in time for pizza.

The Chain Saw Realtor

dam's first week working at the H&R Block office in Boise, Idaho, couldn't have come at a better time. Tax season was just under way and the office was swamped with work. Adam was extremely anxious to dive in and start working, since it had been three months since his last job.

Bob, a seasoned Block veteran, was Adam's mentor. Bob always did his best to make sure a tax preparer did things correctly. Adam was Bob's favorite recruit; He had all the energy needed to get through the long hours of tax season.

"Adam," Bob said, "a client who's a real estate agent will be here at eleven this morning. Would you like to prepare his return?"

"Sure, Bob," Adam eagerly replied. "This will be my first time preparing a real estate agent's return. It's likely I'll have some questions for you."

"No problem. You'll do just fine." Bob reassured him.

Although Adam was swamped with work for the next two hours, he had no problems whatsoever. He felt as if he was on a roll the way he whizzed through his clients' returns.

At precisely eleven o'clock, a forest-green BMW station wagon drove into the parking space in front of the office. It was the real estate agent. A tall, handsome man climbed leisurely out of the car and strolled up to the front door. With a remote-control on his key chain, the man casually locked the car doors and activated a noisy alarm.

He came inside and introduced himself as Hugh Clements. Adam offered Clements a seat and began glancing over the client's paperwork, which included an entire file labeled deductions.

There was more than the normal share of debatable deductions. "I see you list a $400 compact disc player for your car," Adam noted.

"Well," said Clements, "with all the land being developed in the hills, it is sometimes necessary to drive my clients a good half hour to see property. To create a favorable atmosphere, I have to supply them the right music. They are making one of the biggest decisions of their lives. I have to set the mood—you know, relax them."

Adam continued through the list, raising his eyebrows every now and then. Just when he thought Clements had listed every deduction possible, he came across a $275 chain saw. "How does a chain saw fit into your realty business?" Adam asked.

The man chuckled a few times, cleared his throat, and said, "Well, I know it may sound a little strange, but my vehicle has to be in immaculate condition all the time."

"What does that have to do with a chain saw?" Adam questioned.

"Like I was saying, since I spend considerable time driving my clients around in my car, and I like to keep it immaculate, well, I had to buy the chain saw to cut down a pine tree next to my driveway. You see, there was a bird nest up there I couldn't get down. And the birds kept defecating on my car. I couldn't possibly drive clients around in a car with bird-doo all over it, now, could I?"

"Well, I guess not. But that may not warrant deducting a $275 chain saw that was used just once."

A sad look came over the real estate agent's face—the same look that he probably got when a contract fell through on a million-dollar home. He looked over innocently at Adam. "Does this mean I can't deduct the wheelbarrow either?"

A Taxing Matter

ello, H&R Block," Shelley answered the phone in her usual enthusiastic tone. "May I help you?"

"I hope you can, dear," a sweet little voice said. "I came in last year, and my return was done by a very helpful person. My problem is that now it's that time of year again, but I just can't seem to remember the name of my regular taxidermist."

How H&R Block Was Named

H&R Block, the world's largest tax-return preparer, was founded by brothers Henry and Richard Bloch in 1946. Because it was a service business, they believed the company should bear their name. However, they dropped the "h" and added a "k" to their firm's last name to avoid mispronunciations. They didn't want people to say their return was "blotched."

Midnight Run

A few years ago, the main post office in Fort Wayne, Indiana, had a practice of staying open until three A.M. on April 16 to accept letters from taxpayers addressed to the Internal Revenue Service. Postal workers would then backdate the postmark on each envelope to the fifteenth. Understanding that this was the way the post office handled last-minute returns, many taxpayers readily took advantage of it.

One taxpayer in particular who did was Jim Henry.

Henry considered filing his return a distasteful obligation, so he always put off filing for as long as he possibly could. Fred Foster, the local H&R Block office manager, had learned from experience to wait for Henry's late April 15 call.

Generally, around 11:15 P.M. the phone would

ring and Henry would tell Foster: "I'm ready to bring it in for you to work on."

"You're cutting it pretty close again, Jim, aren't you?" Foster would say. "You better get right on over here."

"Will mine be the last return H&R Block does in Fort Wayne?" Henry would always ask.

"It looks that way, Jim."

"Well, if I'm not, I'll just wait a bit longer," he'd answer.

Perhaps it was a game to Jim Henry, but each year, he was the last H&R Block client to file his return in the entire city of Fort Wayne, Indiana. This was a distinction of which he was obviously very proud.